Reforming Metropolitan Governments:
A Bibliography

Garland Reference Library of Social Science (Vol. 12)

Reforming Metropolitan Governments: A Bibliography

Anthony G. White

Garland Publishing, Inc., New York & London

1975

72548

Copyright © 1975 Anthony G. White

Library of Congress Cataloging in Publication Data

White, Anthony G
   Reforming metropolitan governments.

   (Garland reference library of social science ; no. 12)
   1. Metropolitan government--United States--Bib-
liography. I. Title.
Z7164.L8W47 [JS422] 016.352'0094'0973 75-12667
ISBN 0-8240-9994-X

Printed in the United States of America

TABLE OF CONTENTS

TABLES AND FIGURES

1

While the origins and precise nature of "the urban problem" are still open to debate, many of the characteristics of its components are well-known. Overcrowding in central areas, decay of core physical plants, blight, leap-frog zoning, crime, social disorder, voter disenchantment and apathy, alienation from government, and a lack of basic and support services (or an inefficient delivery system for them) all appear as segments of "the urban problem."

Central cities' responses to such issues have typically centered around an attempt to expand their economic resource bases and an expansion of control through annexation, extra-territorial control, or contractual/cooperative agreements with the governments around them. The American city experience has been that these measures only temporarily address the problems at hand, and in fact provide few permanent solutions at all.

A large measure of the blame for "the urban problem" can

be assigned to the maze of governments usually found in urban areas. Counties, created by the states to carry out state administrative functions at the local level, have in many instances become home-rule agencies providing services of purely local concern. Cities, also originally creatures of the state, have in large part become home-rule chartered agencies in order to fulfill their citizens' needs. Surrounding and overlapping the cities are myriads of single- and multiple-purpose district governments which provide schools, fire-protection, water, storm drainage, sanitary sewage disposal, protection from insect-borne disease, and other services. Table 1 summarizes the maze of local governments found in the United States during the period 1962-1972:

Table 1
Units of Local Government, 1962-1972

	1962	1967	1972
STATES	50	50	50
COUNTIES	3,043	3,049	3,044
MUNICIPALITIES	18,000	18,048	18,516
DISTRICTS & TOWNSHIPS	70,143	60,151	56,657
	91,236	81,298	78,267

Source: U.S. Census Bureau, Census of Governments

The number of governments in urban areas fluctuate over time both in size and scope, as the central city annexes more and more territory. As a result, jurisdictional disputes frequently arise over who is - or should be - responsible for providing services to a particular segment of the population. Such disputes tend to be nonproductive and dissipative of resources needed elsewhere.

Nor has there been a lack of proposed reforms to attack the jurisdictional problem. In this context, "reform" is taken in its literal sense, that of the changing of form in adaptation to changing circumstances.

Some small towns contract out all services, hiring their performance through other governmental agencies or private firms. This scheme is popularly known as the "Lakewood Plan," and seems to work if there is a larger governmental entity present willing to do the job.

A municipalized county, or "urban county," can work well as a metropolitan government - at least, so claim reformers. Miami-Dade County, Florida, is the only major county which has adopted this form by voter approval, and it provides several municipal-type services in the areas of the many cities and small towns within its boundaries. Charter provisions also allow Miami-Dade County to accept the responsibility of performing certain other services, should they voluntarily be surrendered by the cities and towns.

Some cities merge with others to provide a uniform base of services financed by a combined tax base. For example, in the period 1867-1911, six cities merged with Boston, Massachusetts. Winchester and Einsted, Connecticut merged in 1961, as did Tampa and Port Tampa, Florida. In a merger, one city agrees to surrender its identity to become a part of another, and thus one entity maintains a legal continuity throughout the proceedings - a factor which can become vital in court cases.

Still another proposed solution is federation, a solution which has not gained acceptance by the voters in the U.S. Under a federated system, services in an urban area - which might extend over several counties - would be functionally divided between an area-wide government and the smaller-area cities (or sub-city areas). The Canadian metropolitan municipalities of Toronto and New Brunswick exemplify the federated concept.

As reform tools, the preceeding plans have had either no or very limited acceptance in the United States. Leaving aside the administrative shuffling generally associated with reform (i.e., abolition of a commission form of government in favor of the council-manager plan, or moving about divisions within departments), the concepts of the city-county and of consolidation represent the reformers' mainstay and major thrust in metropolitan areas.

2

City-counties are, as the name implies, governmental
bodies with the powers and duties of cities and the powers
and duties of counties. Those powers and duties will vary
from state to state, but the basic definition holds
constant across the nation. As such, city-counties can be
created either by separation of a municipality from the
county which surrounds it or by the consolidation of a city
and county.

Separated city-counties have without exception been
created by state legislative processes. There were 36
separated city-counties in the United States in 1972. In
addition to the 33 "independent" cities of Virginia (which
automatically are separated from their counties when the
municipal population reaches 10,000), the cities of
Baltimore (in 1851), San Francisco (1856),[1] and St. Louis
(1876) have all been separated from the counties that had
original jurisdiction over them. The 33 Virginia cities do

<u>not</u> include the four consolidated city-counties found in that state.

Separated Virginia cities are permitted to annex the territory of surrounding counties, while the consolidated city-counties in Virginia are not. Separation as a technique of local government reorganization for the purpose of solving metropolitan problems is discussed elsewhere.[2]

Consolidation involves the dissolution of two or more organizations, the debts, assets, duties and obligations of which are assumed by an entirely new organization created an instant after the dissolution of the participating organizations. It should be obvious that while in a merger one entity can "blend in" the functions and assets of another entity, consolidation requires a great deal of study and preparation - including a constitutional document with clear transition provisions - before the consolidation itself takes place.

One of the major drawbacks to city-county consolidation is that, since the advent of home rule for cities and counties, a referendum must be held on the question of combining the two separate types of governments. Table 2 on the following pages summarizes the track record of consolidation votes. Only 12 of the 58 separate votes have resulted in the creation of a consolidated city-county (the Nansemond and Suffolk/ Nansemond votes related to the same city-county, eventually named "Suffolk"). These 58 referenda were held in 44 cities,

Table 2
Referenda on City-County Consolidation

1921: Oakland/Alameda Co., Cal.
1924: Butte/Silver Bow Co., Mont.
1926: St. Louis/St. Louis Co., Mo.
1929: Pittsburgh/Alleghenny Co., Pa.
1932: Ravalli Co./Several Towns, Mont.
1933: Macon/Bibb Co., Ga.
1935: Jacksonville/Duval Co., Fla.
1947: **Baton Rouge/East Baton Rouge Parish, La.
1948: Birmingham/Jefferson Co., Ala.
Miami/Dade Co., Fla.
1950: Hampton/Newport News/ Elizabeth City Co., Va.
1952: **Hampton/Elizabeth City Co., Va.
1953: Miami/Dade Co., Fla.
1954: Albany/Dougherty Co., Ga.
1958: Nashville/Davidson Co., Tenn.
1959: Albuquerque/Bernalillo Co., N.M.
Knoxville/Knox Co., Tenn.
1960: Macon/Bibb Co., Ga.
1961: Durham/Durham Co., N.C.
Richmond/Henrico Co., Va.
1962: **Nashville/Davidson Co., Tenn.
Columbus/Muscogee Co., Ga.
**Virginia Beach/Princess Anne Co., Va.
**South Norfolk/Norfolk Co., Va.
Memphis/Shelby Co., Tenn.
St. Louis/St. Louis Co., Mo.
1964: Chattanooga/Hamilton Co., Tenn.
1967: Tampa/Hillsborough Co., Fla.
**Jacksonville/Duval Co., Fla.

1969: Athens/Clarke Co., Ga.
**Carson City/Ormsby Co., Nev.
Brunswick/Glynn Co., Ga.
1970: Anchorage/Greater Anchorage Borough, Alas.
Juneau/Greater Juneau Borough, Alas.
**Columbus/Muscogee Co., Ga.
Chattanooga/Hamilton Co., Tenn.
Tampa/Hillsborough Co., Fla.
**Juneau/Greater Juneau Borough, Alas.
Pensacola/Escambia Co., Fla,
Winchester/Frederick Co., Va.
1971: Anchorage/Greater Anchorage Borough, Alas.
Memphis/Shelby Co., Tenn.
**Sitka/Greater Sitka Borough, Alas.
Charlotte/Mecklenburg Co., N.C.
Tallahassee/Leon Co., Fla.
**Nansemond Co./Several Towns, Va.
1972: Tampa/Hillsborough Co., Fla.
**Suffolk/Nansemond City-County, Va.
Columbia/Richland Co., S.C.
Ft. Pierce/St. Lucie Co., Fla.
**Lexington/Fayette Co., Ky.
1973: Tallahassee/Leon Co., Fla.
Savannah/Chatham Co., Ga.
Wilmington/New Hanover Co., N.C.

(Continued)

13

Table 2
(Continued)

1973: Albuquerque/Bernalillo
     Co., N.M.
1974: Durham/Durham Co., N.C.

1974: Portland/Multnomah Co.,
     Ore.
     Sacramento/Sacramento
     Co., Cal.

** Successful referenda.

in a total of 17 states. Five of the 12 city-counties created
by a vote of the people were approved at the second vote on
the measure, sometimes after drastic revision of the first
charter proposed.

In addition to the 12 consolidated city-counties created
by referenda, seven consolidated governments have come into
being through the actions of higher-level governments. These
seven include: Nantucket, Massachusetts; New Orleans, Louisiana; Philadelphia, Pennsylvania; New York, New York; Denver,
Colorado; Honolulu, Hawaii; and Indianapolis-Marion County
(UNIGOV), Indiana.

The only glaring omission from this list is Boston,
Massachusetts. Boston has grown over the centuries, through
annexation and merger with other cities, to almost completely
encompass Suffolk County. Boston's city council acts within
its boundaries as a county court. However, three small towns
(which have rejected merger with Boston) still exist within
Suffolk County's boundaries, and their city councils act as
county commissioners within their respective jurisdictions.
Thus, in terms of scope, authority, area and population,

Boston cannot be said to be a true city-county, consolidated or separated.[3]

The rationales for and against consolidation are brought out for each campaign, altered suitably to fit the local circumstances. In considering the data presented on the following pages, the reader should keep these arguments in mind.

Proponents say that consolidation: will provide a base for uniform, coordinated, planned and financed programs of service delivery; increases the visibility of responsible individuals and agencies in government; enables effective utilization of economies of scale for services, material and administrative overhead; eliminates artificial governmental boundaries; provides responsible government for all services; reduces intergovernmental conflicts; promotes efficiency and effectiveness by eliminating governmental units and overlapping of service areas; broadens the tax base and other resource bases of the agency charged with providing service; eliminates outmoded and inadequate governmental structures; enables establishment of uniform charges for services received, such as water and sewer service; saves interest money paid to bond-holders, since a larger city-county can usually get a better bond rating; is more attractive to federal fund-granting agencies like the U.S. Department of Housing and Urban Development.

Opponents say that consolidation: cannot automatically

15

solve multi-county problems involving the entire metropolitan
area; will face great resistence from existing governments and
their employees; creates a bigger bureaucracy that puts more
people on the public payroll; imposes a "big brother" government on suburban and rural areas; reduces local participation
and local control; cannot deal with rural problems in the same
manner as urban problems; forces suburban codes (building,
electrical, etc.) to be brought up to the level of the central
city; forces a government on suburbanites that they fled the
central city to avoid; is a tool of bussing proponents (or of
the communits/socialist movement); tends to create more problems than it solves.

Of course, city-county consolidation need not be total
in character for the participating agencies to gain some bene-
fit. Many cities and counties share planning services, jails,
library systems; health departments; computer facilities, and
even city-county buildings. Such agreements are usually
contractual in nature, and need not be submitted to the voters
for prior approval.

As for those governments which have completely consolidated, it is of interest to consider a brief historical sketch of
each. In some cases the historical data is incomplete, but a
feel for the development of the consolidation movement can be
attained from that which is available.[4]

NANTUCKET, MASSACHUSETTS: Once a major whaling port, this
community was incorporated in 1687, while under the jurisdic-

16

tion of the New York Colony, and was ceded to the Massachusetts Bay Colony in 1692. While the details are hazy, two prominent families on the island vied for political control, and one side finally gained enough influence in the English Parliament to have a charter granted giving them control over both county and town politics. In 1695, the General Court of Massachusetts recognized the island as a separate county, and the combining of county and town offices took place. Over the years state statutes have completed the task of consolidating the services provided for the community.

NEW ORLEANS, LOUISIANA: Settled by the French, the city of New Orleans was incorporated shortly after the Louisiana Purchase. During the same legislative session of 1805, the territorial legislators created parishes to act as county-type agencies for the performance of territorial services. The territorial legislators apparently thought that their control over the largest and busiest port in the South would be strengthened by making the city and parish coterminous, and so Orleans Parish was given the same boundaries as the city, and parish and city offices were for the most part combined into correspondingly single agencies.

PHILADELPHIA, PENNSYLVANIA: The race riots and civil disorders of the 1840's left many Philadelphians with a sense of helplessness over their own safety, as they could not bring enough resources to bear on control of the problem. The only way to involve the state government in maintaining control was

17

to make Philadelphia coterminous with county boundaries, and city officers to be given the same powers to call on the governor for help as county officers. The Act of Consolidation of 1854 did this, combining 28 of 29 area governments into the City and County of Philadelphia. This consolidation did not, of course, prevent corruption or civil disorder within the city-county, and the powers and administrative combinations were eroded away over the years by Pennsylvania courts and state legislatures. In 1949, a home-rule provision was passed by state voters which allowed Philadelphia voters to adopt a home-rule charter re-consolidating city and county governments. While this charter has held up better than previous ones under court scrutiny, there is still some evidence that some state officers will still be considered as "county" officers.

NEW YORK, NEW YORK: The population of New York City in the 1880's and early 1890's was a diverse, low-income mixture of nationalities, and the counties contiguous to New York were incapable of financing needed facilities for the rapidly-growing neighborhoods. Part of the Bronx had been annexed to New York in 1874, and the rest was annexed in 1895. The citizens of New York, under the Home Rule Charter of 1894, had voted to consolidate with Brooklyn. However, the mayors of New York and Brooklyn could not agree upon a consolidation charter which would satisfy the party machines' in each city. In May of 1897, a charter was agreed upon, but the effective

18

date of the consolidation was postponed indefinately. In
1898 the state legislature was pressured (both by municipal
reformers and the New York 'machine' boss) into enacting
the consolidation charter combining New York, Brooklyn, Richmond, Kings and Queens into the city of Greater New York.

DENVER, COLORADO: Following a failure to consolidate
with Arapahoe County, the government of the city of Denver
lobbied the Colorado State Legislature for creation of a
county around the city into which it could easily expand to
meet the needs of its growing population. In 1901, passage
of an amendment to the state constitution, Article XX, was
executed by the voters which carved out parts of Arapahoe and
Adams Counties to form the County of Denver and consolidate
it with the city. The amendment took effect in 1902, and three
years later a charter was adopted. Since that time, 170
annexations have added over 80 square miles to the territory
of the City and County of Denver.

HONOLULU, HAWAII: Following Hawaii's annexation to the
United States in 1898, no local governments of any kind exist-
ed until 1905. In that year, the County of Oahu was established by the Territorial Legislature to govern the entire
island of Oahu. Following a series of lawsuits brought over
the powers delegated to Oahu County, the 1907 Territorial
Legislature abolished the County and created in its place the
City and County of Honolulu, which encompasses the entire
island. The Mayor-Board of Supervisors form established in

19

1907 was finally superceded by the Mayor-Council form in the charter of 1959.

BATON ROUGE, LOUISIANA: In 1945, Baton Rouge had a population of 35,000 within an area of about five square miles. The last major improvement of public facilities had been in the period 1924-1925. Totally unprepared for the post-war growth that hit many Southern cities, Baton Rouge had grown to over 70,000 population by 1948. The strain was too much for the fiscal and governmental system, and in order to eliminate outmoded governmental structures and attain the tax base necessary to survive as a city, consolidation was proposed. The vote was a slim 51% in favor of consolidation, a margin of only 300 votes in some 13,700 cast.

HAMPTON, VIRGINIA: Hampton was one of the independent cities of Virginia separated from its county. In 1951, the city of Newport News had suggested the consolidation of Hampton, Newport News, and other adjacent jurisdictions to cope with the population-services problems. The suggestion was rejected. At that point, Newport News was threatening to annex the territory surrounding Hampton under Virginia's annexation-by-court-suit law. As a consequence, Elizabeth City County, the town of Phoebus, and the City of Hampton voted to consolidate in 1952, in order to avoid the higher tax rates imposed in Newport News. The county of Warwick, surrounding Newport News, incorporated and became a city in the same election. Warwick and Newport News came together in a city-

city consolidation four years later.

NASHVILLE, TENNESSEE: Nashville was caught up in the same rapid influx of population following World War II as many other southern U.S. cities. Many of these immigrants settled outside the city limits in Davidson County, thus overloading the antiquated facilities of the county. A 1951 report of the Tennessee Taxation Association recommended complete consolidation of the city and county. A Tennessee statute enacted in 1955 permitted cities to annex without a referendum, and in defense three new cities were incorporated in Davidson County during the period 1957-1959. In 1958, following a battle in the state legislature over an enabling act to allow a consolidation vote, the ensuing vote denied Nashville and Davidson County the act of consolidation by a 6-to-5 margin.

In 1960, Nashville annexed 42 square miles of Davidson County, containing 80,000 people, without submitting the question to a vote. Understandably some citizens were upset by this move, considering that urban-type services did not appear to be developed enough for extension to them, and a new movement was begun to consolidate in order to oust the mayor and his council. A vote on the issue in 1962 favored consolidation by a 4-to-3 margin, with a 50% higher turnout than in 1958.

VIRGINIA BEACH, VIRGINIA: Using Virginia's annexation-without-referenda law, the city of Norfolk had, in 1959,

21

annexed 13 square miles and 38,000 people from Princess Anne County. Fearful of being cut off from all possible expansion, and of being subjected to the higher tax rates of Norfolk, the voters of Virginia Beach and Princess Anne County moved to cut off Norfolk's expansion by voting in 1963 to consolidate.

CHESAPEAKE, VIRGINIA: Prevented from expansion into Princess Anne County, Norfolk turned to Norfolk County for territory into which it could grow. The citizens of South Norfolk, themselves not wanting to be prevented from growth, convinced the Norfolk County voters that tax rates with South Norfolk would remain considerably lower than in Norfolk. A 1962 vote authorized the consolidation of South Norfolk and Norfolk County, which became effective in 1963. Following adoption of the charter, a referendum was held on the name for the new city, and the name "Chesapeake" was selected.

JACKSONVILLE, FLORIDA: A 1956 study explored the possibility of city-county consolidation in Florida, with particular reference to Miami and Jacksonville. A decline in central-city population coupled with a corresponding increase in suburban population brought financial stress to the city of Jacksonville in the 1960's. Jacksonville had a mayor-council/city commission form of government, and had publicly identified as problems duplication of services and fragmentation and overlapping of jurisdictions with Duval County. Against this backdrop, Jacksonville's schools were disaccredi-

22

ted in 1965, and several government officials were brought before a grand jury on charges of corruption in 1966 (several were later convicted). In August, 1967, a referendum to consolidate Jacksonville and Duval County resulted in a 54,500 to 29,700 vote favoring consolidation. The new government became legally effective in October of 1968.

CARSON CITY, NEVADA: The charter of Carson City, Nevada was amended in 1951 to combine the offices of Clerk, Auditor, Assessor, District Attorney, and Sheriff with the corresponding offices of Ormsby County. In the period 1964-1968 a functional consolidation of most of the other service departments took place. The city council and county commissioners of Ormsby County had long been in agreement that total consolidation was in order for a geographically small, isolated area, and would make stretching of available funds possible. A statewide election amending the state's constitution in 1968 approved the formal consolidation of the two units, and in that year their governments were combined under a legislatively-drafted charter.

INDIANAPOLIS, INDIANA: The consolidation of Indianapolis and Marion County is considered to be the work of one man - Mayor Richard Lugar. He was elected to office in 1967, the first Republican to hold the mayor's office in many decades. Indianapolis suffered many of the ills of urban areas - declining central-city population, racial tensions, declining purchasing power provided by a static tax base, and ineffici-

23

ency through duplication of services and overlapping of jursidictions with Marion County. Using the prestige of his office, Mayor Lugar and the strong Marion County Republican Party convinced the state legislature (also strongly Republican at that time) that consolidation was necessary for the continued operation of the city. The Legislature, which serves as a second city council for Indianapolis, agreed with the Mayor and approved a consolidation bill which was signed in March of 1969. The law had an emergency clause which made the consolidation effective in January of 1970, and which exempted from the consolidation the towns of Speedway, Beach Grove, and Lawrence.

JUNEAU, ALASKA: Founded as a gold-rush center in 1881, Juneau as the capital of Alaska has spawned many innovative precepts of state and local government. The Greater Juneau Borough covers 3,000 square miles, but contains only 13,000 people, and so the mechanism of consolidation was nurtured in the state constitution and statutes, just in case it was needed to cope with adjusting service levels for a small population spread out over a large area. When in 1970 Juneau residents became disenchanted with their current administration's actions and policies, consolidation was proposed and approved (on the second try), and the consolidated unit is considered to be both a city and borough under Alaska law.

COLUMBUS, GEORGIA: School administration functions of Columbus and Muscogee County were merged in 1948, followed by

water, sewer, and airport facilities in the 1950's and 1960's.
A formal consolidation of the two governmental units was
defeated in 1962. Nearly all council members and the mayor
were replaced in the election of 1964, and a study commission
was authorized by the Georgia General Assembly in 1966 to
prepare a new consolidation plan. Following an active,
"grass-roots" campaign, a 1970 vote approved consolidation
by 10,000 votes (with only a 30% turnout of registered voters).

SITKA, ALASKA: The policies of the pre-consolidation
mayor did not sit very well with many Sitka residents.
In an area whose economy depends upon fishing, lumbering and
tourism - no one of which contributes substantially to the
assessed value which generates the tax base - services could
neither be uniformly expanded nor proportionally paid for.

With the example of Juneau's unification just across
the straights, Sitka citizens saw solutions to their problems
in consolidation. In 1971, a charter was drafted and adopted
by a large majority of the voters.

SUFFOLK, VIRGINIA: Nansemond County in 1971 was faced
with a large-scale annexation of its territory by the independent city of Suffolk. Following the lead of neighboring
Chesapeake and Virginia Beach, the county's civic leaders
proposed a consolidation of the county, the city of Suffolk,
and the towns of Holland and Whaleyville. When the Suffolk
city council refused to allow the consolidation question to
appear on the city ballot, the voters of the county and the

two small towns agreed to consolidate and become the City-County of Nansemond - a city-county whose city hall was located in the independent city of Suffolk.

Suffolk's annexation suit was pressed in the courts. As a reaction to this case and other pending charter commissions in Virginia, the General Assembly passed a statute declaring a moratorium on annexations, incorporations, and the creation of new city-counties (see Appendix II).

Faced with a court battle on the question of annexation, and just ahead of the effective date of the moratorium statute, Suffolk consolidation advocates obtained a court order placing the question of Suffolk-Nansemond consolidation on the city's ballot. The consolidation agreement was adopted at the polls on November 2, 1972, and became effective on January 1, 1974.

LEXINGTON, KENTUCKY: Lexington's vigorous annexation policies in the 1950's and 1960's created a city boundary that gave planners and policy-makers nightmares. Continuous conflicts arose between city and county agencies over who had jurisdiction when police and fire services were needed. In 1969, Lexington won an annexation suit which would have annexed to the city large pieces of territory and more than 50,000 people between 1975 and 1980. Intergovernmental conflicts, budget crises, and pending lawsuits against the city became commonplace, creating an atmosphere of steady panic in city government. One council member in 1970 was

tried - and acquited - on bribery charges. A 1971 city
council reform ticket was elected to office, and spearheaded
the consolidation campaign to its successful conclusion in
1972. The consolidated government became the governing
agency of the area on January 1, 1974.

This brief discussion cannot, of course, begin to cover
the finer points of pre-consolidation conditions or campaign
tactics in each consolidation. For a more in-depth look at
a particular consolidation, the reader is referred to the
subject index at the end of this text.

However, having now been presented with an overview of
the types of conditions surrounding city-county consolidations,
the reader should now be ready for harder data concerning
the city-counties themselves.

Notes:

1. While the City and County of San Francisco is often held
up as an example of city-county consolidation, a reading of
the Act involved (see reference 473) shows that, in combining
the two governments, the California Legislature split off an
area from the original San Francisco County, coterminous with
the city, to create the city-county. The remainder territory
became San Mateo County, making San Francisco an example of
city-county separation.

2. In particular, see references 11 and 104.

3. See references 129 and 130.

4. A map showing the geographic distribution of consolidated
city-counties is found in Appendix I. These brief paragraphs
are distillates of published documents found in this bibliography, surveys conducted by the author and the Portland-
Multnomah County City-County Charter Commission, and interview
with public officials in several of the city-counties.

3

This chapter will for the most part be tabular, and the author will not attempt to provide long-winded interpretations of the data. In fact, the reader is invited to draw a random sample of cities (controlling for, say, size or geographic location) and devising the comparable data and statistical tests to check for significant differences. The main purpose of this text is to provide a general profile of metropolitan areas that have chosen to approach the reform of their governments through city-county consolidation.

Of all the possible characteristics to consider, the ones singled out here center around geographic, demographic, social, economic, political, service-related, and charter document factors. Also, the data presented will be for the 13 city-counties formed after 1947, the reason being that no pre-consolidation data is available for the city-counties formed during the period 1695-1947.

Table 3 outlines the city-county land areas, the change

in the land's primary agricultural use over a five-year span,
and any special features of the city-counties' location:

Table 3
City-County Geographic Features

	1974 Land Area[a]	% Change, Land in Farms, 1964-69	Special Features
Baton Rouge	459	− 12.4	--
Hampton	55	--	Port
Nashville	508	− 0.7	--
Chesapeake	343	− 11.4	--
Virginia Beach	259	− 16.7	--
Jacksonville	766	− 15.5	Port
Carson City	140	− 66.8	Mountain-Valley
Indianapolis	392	− 10.2	--
Columbus	220	− 19.5	On State Boundary
Juneau	1,286	--	On State Boundary/Port
Sitka	2,296	--	Island
Suffolk	408	− 11.2	--
Lexington	280	− 2.4	--

a. In square miles. Water area omitted.

Few cities in the United States cover more than 100 square
miles in area, yet 12 of these 13 city-counties exceed that
level. This should indicate the special problems encountered
by a city-county in trying to provide services like sewage
treatment and fire protection. It is also interesting to note
that primary-use land is being rapidly converted from agricultural use to some other form, and that some city-counties
occupy special geographic positions of isolation and/or trans-

portation importance. Indeed, of the six city-counties not
considered in table 3, three are wholly or partially contained
on islands, four are major ports, and one is set apart by
high desert plateau isolation.

Demographically, the population, population changes, and
non-white population all reflect migratory patterns to and
from consolidated city-counties, and are indicative of
opportunities perceived to be available to immigrants and em-
migrants. Also included in the following table is the total
crime index for 1972, which can be indicative of several
economic, racial, and other factors better discussed in the
FBI's Uniform Crime Report:

Table 4
Demographic Aspects of City-Counties

	1970 Population (in 1000s)	% Change in Population 1960-1970	Blacks as % of Total Pop. 1960	1970	1972 Crime Index[a]
Baton Rouge	162	6.6	31.7	28.7	10486
Hampton	119	-33.7	21.1	25.3	2514
Nashville	444	159.6	19.1	19.6	17017
Chesapeake	89	20.3	26.1	23.1	2335
Virginia Beach	166	95.3	15.2	9.1	4368
Jacksonville	513	155.2	23.2	22.4	22975
Carson City	15	199.6	0.9	1.0	590
Indianapolis	743	56.1	6.5	17.0	19207
Columbus	152	30.0	23.9	25.6	3906
Juneau	13	--	--	--	na [b]
Sitka	6	22.0	--	--	na
Suffolk	35	12.0	63.0	54.1	na
Lexington	174	32.2	15.2	12.3	5059

a. Measured in crimes per 100,000 population.
b. na = not available.

As table 4 shows, consolidated city-counties range
from 6 thousand to over 700 thousand in population (almost
eight million when New York is considered). While large
population increases are indicated during the decade of the
1960s, this is in large part due to the Census Bureau's
comparison with the old, unconsolidated city's population.
The black population as a proportion of the overall total
fluctuates widely with each city-county, and the crime index
does also.

Some social characteristics of the populations of consoli
dated city-counties are also of interest. The percentage of
all families at the poverty level (arbitrarily set at $3000
annually), the educational level of the citizenry, and the
percentage of all workers employed in white-collar occupations
may provide keys as to why or why not a metropolitan area may
choose city-county consolidation over some other method of
governmental reform. Of course, the first and third factors
could just as well be considered economic characteristics, but
for the purposes of this text will be considered social factor

Table 5 on the following page shows a marked decline in
the number of families earning under $3000 annually over the
decade of 1960-1970. Likewise, education levels are uniformly
higher, and the number of workers in white-collar categories
increases in each city-county over the same ten-year period.
Once again, this could be attributed to the inclusion of
former suburbs in the city-county jurisdiction, or it could

Table 5
Sociometric Characteristics of City-Counties

	% of Families Below Poverty Level		Median Education		% Workers White Collar	
	1960	1970	1960	1970	1960	1970
Baton Rouge	21.9	11.7	11.9	12.3	46.7	54.2
Hampton	15.5	8.0	11.8	12.1	46.8	52.9
Nashville	23.5	9.4	10.3	12.0	45.9	54.4
Chesapeake	21.7	8.9	9.6	10.7	36.8	41.9
Virginia Beach	22.2	8.3	12.0	12.4	48.7	61.3
Jacksonville	22.4	12.4	10.8	12.0	45.4	53.6
Carson City	11.9	6.1	12.4	12.6	53.4	64.1
Indianapolis	12.8	11.7	11.4	12.2	46.8	52.5
Columbus	27.7	13.9	10.2	12.0	41.1	50.3
Juneau	na	3.0	na	12.7	na	73.9
Sitka	na	2.5	na	12.4	na	46.0
Suffolk	43.8	15.7	7.5	9.5	21.6	30.6
Lexington	23.6	9.0	11.2	12.3	47.8	57.3

---

na = not available.

be a part of a national trend, or it could be a unique charac-
teristic of consolidated city-counties.

The economic data presented in table 6 is slightly
altered as it came from the original sources to prevent
infringement. In the area of bonds, a rating of 1 will be
considered the best attainable (and therefore the most attractive to investors) and a rating of 10 will be the worst. With
regard to the city-counties' basic economic functions, the
following scale will hold: 10 = primary agricultural activities; 9 = secondary agricultural activities; 8 = transportation; 7 = manufacturing; 6 = wholesaling; 5 = retailing; 4 =
government; 3 = finance; 2 = service industries; and 1 = a
diversified economy.

Table 6
Econometric Characteristics of City-Counties

	General Obligation Bond Rating		Major Economic	1972 Local Tax Rates [a]	
	Precon.	Postcon.	Function(s)	Sales	Income
Baton Rouge	5	3	1,4	3.0	--
Hampton	4	4	8	1.0	--
Nashville	2	2	1,3,4	1.5	--
Chesapeake	5	4	8	1.0	--
Virginia Beach	5	4	8	1.0	--
Jacksonville	4	3	2,3,7	--	--
Carson City	5	5	4	0.5	--
Indianapolis	2	1	1,3,4	--	--
Columbus	3	3	1,7	--	--
Juneau	5	5	4,8	3.0	--
Sitka	5	5	2,7,9	3.0	--
Suffolk	4	4	1,6	1.0	--
Lexington	4	4	2,8	--	1.5

a = in percent.

General obligation bonds pledge the full faith and credit
of a city behind a debt, which means that property tax dollars
can be used to pay off the indebtedness. The rating of these
bonds reflects the rater's opinion based on property values,
recent tax collections, debt history, total city revenues, and
many other municipal finance factors, and are thus a good
indicator of a city's (or city-county's) financial health.

As the table indicates, five of the 13 city-counties
considered here have improved their bond ratings since their
respective consolidations took place. The others have remained
constant, an indication of either no improvement or the time
lapse necessary following consolidation for substantial improvements to be made. The basic economic functions which are

34

regularly repeated here are diversified, government, and transportation in nature. Only one of this sample levies an income tax, although both New York and Philadelphia in that part of the unexamined sample levy income taxes.

Table 7 examines some of the political/governmental characteristics of the city-counties and their populations. The number of local governmental units according to the Bureau of the Census comes from the Census of Governments taken every five years. Percentage of Democratic Party voters is from the presidential general elections of 1960 and 1968. "Opted-out towns" are municipal corporations which remained apart from the consolidations, and for which the city-counties must perform county-type services (such as tax collection, maintenance of county roads, etc.). Starred city-counties are also state capitals.

Table 7
Political Characteristics of City-Counties

	# of Local Governments		% Voting for Democratic Party		# of Opted-Out Towns
	1967	1972	1960	1968	
Baton Rouge*	6	6	46.6	27.7	3
Hampton	1	1	48.5	34.7	0
Nashville*	13	15	53.0	32.6	6
Chesapeake	1	4	58.2	28.3	0
Virginia Beach	1	1	55.1	27.0	0
Jacksonville	13	9	54.3	32.8	4
Carson City*	4	5	39.7	43.4	0
Indianapolis*	60	52	42.3	47.7	3
Columbus	6	5	47.2	22.0	1
Juneau*	3	1	na	na	0 **
Sitka	2	1	na	na	0
Suffolk	5	1	74.1	41.6	0
Lexington	10	7	39.6	33.7	0

(table 7, continued)

---

* = State Capital
** = Town of Douglas sued to remain apart from the Juneau-
     Greater Juneau Borough consolidation, but lost in the
     courts and was involuntarily dissolved.

Seven of the 13 city-counties decreased the number of
local governments within their jurisdictions in the five-year
period 1967-1972, while three held the number constant and
three actually increased the number of agencies considered
by the Census Bureau to be "local governments." The drop
in Democratic Party support can in part be attributed to that
portion of the vote drawn off to the American Independent
Party, especially in the Southernmost states.

Three areas of service provision are considered in table
8: fire protection; volume of police protection; and tax
collection. While many citizens do not consider the latter
a "service," it does provide for the general operation of
government and reflects the citizens' acceptance of that
government's legitimacy and right to exist.

Insurance rating bureaus grade fire departments, their
equipment and training, alarm systems, water systems, and
prevention programs to arrive at an overall rating of a city,
which insurance companies then use to arrive at insurance
premium rates. The best achievable is a rating of "1", the
worst is "10" - totally unprotected. Most often, zones are
established in a ring pattern around the central city, each

36

one of which is rated separately. Thus, a city with a rating
of 3/8 would have one zone with a "3" rating and the other
with an "8" rating.

Table 8
Selected Services Provided in City-Counties

	Fire Insurance Ratings		# of Police Per 100,000	% of 1970 Property Tax
	Precon.	Postcon.	Residents	Levy Collected
Baton Rouge	4	2	285	97.8
Hampton	5	2	147	99.1
Nashville	3/10	3/9/10**	183	96.2
Chesapeake	2/10	2/4	215	95.1
Virginia Beach	7/10	7/10	166	93.8
Jacksonville	2/9/10	2/10*	225	97.6
Carson City	5/10	5/9/10**	267	96.8
Indianapolis	2/10	2/10	243	97.4
Columbus	3/7	3/7	200	96.0
Juneau	5/6/10	5/6/10	250	94.1
Sitka	na	na	173	90.0
Suffolk	na	na	94	96.4
Lexington	na	na	160	na

na = not available
* = the "9" area became a part of the "2" area.
** = part of the "10" area improved to a "9" rating

Some city-counties improved fire protection following
consolidation, some did not. Apparently none of them allowed
fire protection service to deteriorate. As for the number
of police per 100,000 population, the national average (according to the FBI) is about 235.

The last table to be presented in this text deals with
some of the charter characteristics of these 13 city-counties.
It is a matter of some importance whether a city-county lies
in a home-rule or non-home-rule state, for it is that factor

which determines who draws up the proposed charter - the state legislature or the citizens themselves. It is also of interest to compare these charters against some standard to see how they "measure up," in this instance against the National Municipal League's Model Charter. Finally, the amount of transition time allowed in the charter for the governments involved to consolidate reflects the complexity of issues which must be addressed between the time of adoption of the charter and the effective date of the new government.

Table 9
Charter Characteristics of Consolidated City-Counties

	Source of Charter		% Congruence to Municipal League Model[a]	# of Months for Transition
	State	Local		
Baton Rouge		X	80	16
Hampton	X		60	½
Nashville		X	92	10
Chesapeake	X		66	10½
Virginia Beach	X		54	10
Jacksonville	X		88	14
Carson City	X		52	2
Indianapolis	X		56	8½
Columbus		X	76	7
Juneau		X	82	4½
Sitka		X	86	4
Suffolk	X		54	14
Lexington		X	94	14

a = A matching of the minimal charter sections in the model to see if they are present in the city-county charters. Of course, many additional charter sections are present in all city-county charters to cover local and unique needs.

Charters drafted by local charter commissions show a much

38

closer match to the "good government" model than do charters
drafted by state legislatures. However, there appears to be
no correlation between local/state drafting and the amount of
time set aside for making the transition from the unconsolidated state to the consolidated one.

Several interesting and innovative charter provisions are
to be found in city-county charters, especially in the areas
of citizen involvement, conflicts of interest, representation,
and keeping the charter up-to-date. Several of these innovative sections are to be found in Appendix III.

Having taken a more in-depth look at the details of some
aspects of the more recent city-county consolidations, a few
generalizations can be made about what constitutes a city-
county. The next chapter will sketch a brief profile of the
metropolitan government reformed by consolidation, based on
chapters 2 and 3.

4

The question at this point should be, " What good does
a profile of consolidated city-counties do?" The answer
should be two-fold: first, it provides a picture of consolidation against which the pros and cons discussed in chapter
2 can be compared to see who (if anyone) was right; and
second, it provides a model against which areas can measure
themselves to see if consolidation might be a worthwhile
reform to consider.

The following description will, then, describe no one
existing city-county, but provides a composite image in very
generalized form. Its usefulness can only be measured by
experience.

A consolidated city-county will be large in land area,
but urbanizing processes will be taking land out of farm
production and replacing it with houses, stores, and factories
It will be unable to expand in one or more directions, because
of island boundaries, the sea, a river, or a state boundary.

The population will be medium-sized, from 100,000 to 500,000 people, with a 10% to 20% non-white segment. The economic condition of the average family will have improved (in an absolute, not relative, sense) over the last decade, and overall education and job status levels will have risen in that same time period.

City-county economy will have been relatively stable with regard to pre-consolidation finances, based upon local economies of transportation, finance, government, and broad-based mixtures of industry. Outside of the property tax, the mainstay of tax revenues for the city-county will be a local sales tax, levied at a rate between 1% and 3% of gross sales.

With the bulk of the newer city-counties in the South, voting patterns will have shifted from support of the Democratic Party to the American Independent Party, in somewhat the same spirit of desire for reform that created the city-counties. Services will have remained stable or improved following consolidation, although a corresponding increase in use charges may accompany service improvements not backed by the property tax.

During the consolidation campaign, some impending crisis will have arisen which threatens the livability of the city or the fabric of government, shaking the confidence of citizens in their city agencies to operate honestly, efficiently, and economically. Perhaps politics outside the metropolitan area has played a major role in the push for consolidation. At any rate, when the issue comes to a vote, the citizenry are more than ready for a change, and consolidation is perhaps a chance to "throw the rascals out."

This text has shown concrete data about what reform is, what it looks like, and what happens when it is adopted – particularly in the case of city-county consolidation, the most frequently adopted metropolitan reform in the United States. This material, and the bibliography which follows, should form the basis for many more questions to be asked and answers to be sought.

APPENDIX I

Geographic Distribution of
Consolidated City-Counties

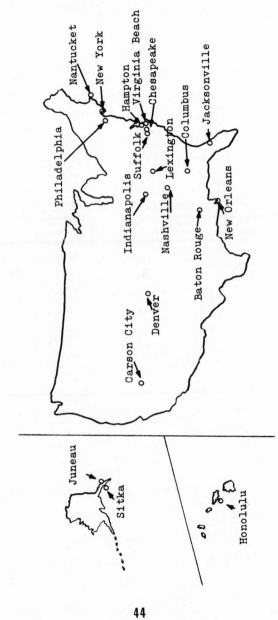

APPENDIX II

Virginia Consolidation Moratorium
and Response

Chapter 712, Acts of Assembly of 1972, General Assembly of
Virginia, April 10, 1972.

Be it enacted by the General Assembly of Virginia:

1. That the second enactment of Chapter 234 of the Acts of
Assembly of 1971 be amended and reenacted as follows:

2. (a) Beginning March one, nineteen hundred seventy-two and
terminating January one, nineteen hundred seventy-six, no
city charter shall be granted or come into force in any county
which adjoins a city and, for and during such time, no annexation suit shall be instituted by a city against any county; an
annexation suit by a city against any county instituted during
such time shall be stayed; provided, however, that an annexation suit against any county instituted and pending prior to
March one, nineteen hundred seventy-two, shall not be stayed
and such proceedings shall continue in any such suit; provided,
however, that the foregoing shall not prohibit the institution
of an annexation proceeding for the purpose of implementing
annexation involving such county, the extent, terms and conditions of which have been agreed upon by such county and a city
or by such county and a town; provided further, that the
foregoing shall not prohibit annexation proceedings under
sections 15.1-1034 of the Code of Virginia; and provided
further, that the foregoing shall not prohibit the consolidation into a city of any county and all the towns located there-
in if the consolidation procedure has been initiated and the
referendum held prior to January 1, 1972.

Excerpts, Letter to Author from Robert C. Fitzgerald, Attorney-
at-Law, dated January 16, 1973, subject: Effects of the above
upon city-county consolidation in Virginia.
Mr. Fitzgerald handled several annexation cases in the Chesapeake and Nansemond consolidations.

". . .In my judgement, these consolidations provided the best
answer to both the cities and counties involved. Cities,
because of the age of the greater part of their development,
tend to look to the newer development and underdeveloped space
in the counties as the answer to their problems. On the other
hand, counties which have already had to gear their governmental
structure to provide for the diversity of services between the
developed areas and rural areas find it detrimental to lose
what is usually the most lucrative part of their revenue and
customer base and find the removal of area, citizens, and
facilities highly disruptive to most functions of government
. . . I doubt that the current moratorium has done anything

more than please the cities who got in under the wire, infuriate the counties subject to those annexation suits, encourage towns and suits by petitioners which are not prohibited. The current moratorium was created initially in a standoff between the Counties of Chesterfield and Henrico in their legislative attempt to obtain charters (in order to prevent further annexations) and the City of Richmond's threatened annexation suit. . . Therefore I would not conclude that the "moratorium" will have any good effect on government reorganization in Virginia."

APPENDIX III

Innovative City-County
Charter Provisions

Differential Taxation

Example: Columbus, Georgia

Section 1-103. Taxing Districts.

(1) The consolidated government shall, within the geographic limits thereof, comprise two or more taxing districts, (herein called 'service districts'), wherein taxes shall be assessed, levied, and collected by the consolidated government in accordance with the kind, character, type, degree, and level of services provided by said government within said services districts, and the rate and manner of taxation may vary in any one district from that in another and other districts. The powers, authority, duties, liabilities, and functions of the consolidated government may vary in any district from that in another or other districts, as provided by ordinance. . .

Representation on City-County Council

Example: Virginia Beach, Virginia

Section 3.01. Division of city into boroughs; composition of council.

The city shall be divided into seven boroughs. One such borough shall comprise the city of Virginia Beach as existing immediately preceeding the effective date of this Charter and shall be known as the borough of Virginia Beach . . .(descriptions of the remaining six boroughs). . . The council shall consist of eleven members, one to be elected by the city at large from among the residents of each of the seven boroughs and four to be elected by and from the city at large. (Emphasis added)

Automatic Review of the Charter

Example: Juneau, Alaska

Section 14.4. Proposal by Charter Commission

(a) Every ten years subsequent to 1970 the clerk shall place on the ballot for the next regular election the question: "Shall there be a Charter Commission to review or amend the Charter?" If a majority of the qualified voters voting on the question vote "no," the question shall not be placed on the ballot until the end of the next ten year period. If a majority of the qualified voters voting on the question vote "yes," nine qualified voters to serve as the Charter Commission shall be chosen at the next regular election or at a special election. The commission members shall be elected on the same basis of representation as assemblymen. A vacancy shall be filled by the commission with a qualified voter representing the same area as the member he succeeds. . .

Citizens' Advocate (Ombudsman)

Example: Lexington, Kentucky

Section 4.11 Citizens' Advocate.

The Council shall, within one year of the effective date of this Charter, create and establish an Office of Citizens' Advocate. It shall be the purpose of said office to provide the citizens of Lexington-Fayette Urban County Government with an independent agent through whom they can seek redress of their grievances. To that end, the Citizens' Advocate shall be empowered to: a) investigate any complaint by citizens of the Urban County Government; b) disclose any abuses or irregularities on the part of the Urban County Government, its officers, agents or employees; and c) recommend such substantive or procedural policies as may be required to reduce or eliminate problems of citizen access to the departments, divisions, agencies and officers of the Urban County Government. . .

BIBLIOGRAPHY

I. Books; Documents; Pamphlets

1. A Future for Nashville. (Nashville: Community Services
Committee for Davidson County and the City of Nashville, 1952).

2. Advisory Commission on Intergovernmental Relations.
Alternative Approaches to Governmental Reorganization
in Metropolitan Areas. (Washington, D.C.: U.S.
Government Printing Office, 1962).

3. ------. County Reform. (Washington, D.C.: U.S. Government
Printing Office, 1971).

4. ------. Factors Affecting Voter Reaction to Government
Reorganization in Metropolitan Areas. (Washington,
D.C.: U.S. Government Printing Office, 1962).

 A classic, often-quoted study of governmental
 reorganization case studies. Included are seven case
 studies of attempted consolidations. The study focus-
 es on the roles of various community elements, and
 examines some support-gathering techniques for
 winning passage of reform measures. The report
 finishes with a good bibliographic source list on the
 cases studied.

5. ------. Governmental Structure, Organization, and Planning
in Metropolitan Areas. (Washington, D.C.: U.S.
Government Printing Office, 1961).

6. ------. Profile of County Government. (Washington, D.C.:
U.S. Government Printing Office, 1971).

 This report presents the results of a survey of
 county governments across the U.S. to determine
 trends in adapting to, and coping with, changing
 political environments. About 40% is devoted to
 consolidations, attempted consolidations and studies
 relating to functional or formal city-county mergers.
 There are a number of qualitative and quantitative
 errors in the work, and its conclusions should be
 approached with caution.

7. ------. Urban America and the Federal System. (Washington, D.C.: U.S. Government Printing Office, 1969).

8. Advisory Committees. Report of Advisory Committees for the
Consolidation of the City of Richmond and Henrico
County. (Richmond, Va.: The Committees, July 1, 1961).

9. Adrian, Charles R. _Governing Urban America_. (New York: McGraw-Hill, 1955). Pp. 283-284.

10. American Society of Planning Officials. _Toward More Effective Planning in Jacksonville_. (Chicago: The Society, 1971).

11. Bain, Charles W. _A Body Incorporate: The Evolution of City-County Separation in Virginia_. (Charlottesville: University of Virginia, 1967).

12. -----. _Annexation in Virginia_. (Charlottesville: University of Virginia, 1966).

13. Bancroft, Caroline. _Denver's Lively Past_. (Boulder: Johnson Publishing Company, 1959).

    While this little booklet was written for the tourist trade, it does mention the Denver consolidation in passing, and discusses in some detail the trials and tribulations of the consolidated government's first mayor.

14. Banovetz, James M., Ed. _Managing the Modern City_. (Washington, D.C.: International City Managers' Association, 1971). Pp. 445-447.

15. Baton Rouge, City of. _Our City-Parish Government: A Thumbnail Sketch_. (Baton Rouge: The City, n.d.).

    A "public service" document written on an elementary level, this pamphlet is the main piece of material distributed to those writing the city for consolidation information.

16. Berry, Brian J.L. and Jack Meltzer. _Goals for Urban America_. (Englewood Cliffs, N.J.: Prentice-Hall, 1967).

17. Bigelow, Page Elizabeth and Judith A. Moncrieff. _Selected Articles on Metropolitan Areas and Governmental Consolidation from the National Civic Review_. (New York: National Municipal League, 1971).

18. Blair, George S. "Analyzing Governmental Structure in a Metropolitan Area with Particular Reference to the Philadelphia Area," in _Metropolitan Analysis_. (Philadelphia: University of Pennsylvania Press, 1958).

19. Board of County Commissioners. Your Multnomah County
    Government Handbook. (Portland: Multnomah County,
    1969).

20. Bollens, John C. "Metropolitan and Fringe Area Develop-
    ments in 1958," in Municipal Year Book.
    (Chicago: International City Managers' Association,
    1959).

21. -----. "Metropolitan and Fringe Area Developments in
    1959," in Municipal Year Book. (Chicago, Inter-
    national City Managers' Association, 1960).

22. -----. "Metropolitan and Fringe Area Developments in
    1960," in Municipal Year Book. (Chicago, Inter-
    national City Managers' Association, 1961).

23. -----. "Metropolitan and Fringe Area Developments in
    1962," in Municipal Year Book. (Chicago, Inter-
    national City Managers' Association, 1963).

24. -----, John R. Bayes, and Kathryn L. Utter. American
    County Government. (Beverly Hills: Sage, 1969).

25. Bollens, John C. and Henry J. Schmandt. The Metropolis:
    Its People, Politics, and Economic Life. (New York:
    Harper and Row, 1965).

26. Booth, David A. Metropolitics: The Nashville Consolida-
    tion. (East Lansing: Institute for Community
    Development, Michigan State University, 1963).

        A historical monograph written about the
    Nashville consolidation. The 1958 failure is
    briefly addressed, and the interim period 1958-1962
    in more closely examined. The bulk of Booth's
    efforts are spent in analyzing a survey of citizen
    attitudes, taken shortly after the 1958 failure -
    a survey which probably aided the proponents during
    the 1962 campaign.

27. Bromage, Arthur W. Political Representation in Metro-
    politan Agencies. (Ann Arbor: University of
    Michigan Institute of Public Administration, 1962).

28. Bureau of Municipal Research and Service. An Introductio
    to Local Government. (Eugene, Oregon: University of
    Oregon, 1971).

29. -----. Local Intergovernmental Cooperation in the Tri-
    County Area. (Eugene, Oregon: University of Oregon,
    November 1966).

30. -----. Selected Data on the Finances of State and Local
    Governments in Oregon - Finance Bulletin No. 9.
    (Eugene: The Bureau, University of Oregon, 1971).

31. Bureau of the Census, U.S. Department of Commerce.
    Census of Population: 1940; 1950; 1960; 1970.
    (Washington, D.C.: U.S. Government Printing Office,
    1941; 1951; 1961; 1971).

32. -----. 1967 Census of Governments: Governmental Organiza-
    tion. (Washington, D.C.: U.S. Government Printing
    Office, 1968).

33. -----. 1972 Census of Governments: Governmental Organiza-
    tion. (Washington, D.C.: U.S. Government Printing
    Office, 1973).

34. -----. County and City Data Book 1967 - A Statistical
    Abstract Supplement. (Washington, D.C.: U.S. Govern-
    ment Printing Office, 1967).

35. Bureau of Public Administration. City Consolidation in
    the Lower Peninsula. (Charlottesville: University
    of Virginia, 1956).

36. Carson City, City of. Historical Data, Legal Require-
    ments, Reasons and Effects of Consolidation of
    Carson City and Ormsby County into a New Entity -
    Carson City, Nevada. (Carson City: The City, n.d.).

37. Chamber of Commerce. Economic Profile: Virginia Beach,
    Virginia. (Virginia Beach: Chamber of Commerce,
    1972).

38. Charlotte-Mecklenburg Charter Commission. Proposed
    Charter for the Consolidated Government of Charlotte
    and Mecklenburg County. (Charlotte, N.C.: The
    Commission, 1971).

39. -----. Responsible Local Government. (Charlotte, N.C.:
    The Commission, 1971).

40. Charter Commission for South Norfolk and Norfolk County,
    Virginia. Shall We Push Together or Shall We
    Surrender Separately? (South Norfolk: The Commis-
    sion, 1962).

41. -----. A Historic Past: A Promising Future. (South
    Norfolk: The Commission, 1961).

42. Chattanooga Chamber of Commerce. Consolidated Government Charter. (Chattanooga: The Chamber, 1970).

43. Chicago Home Rule Commission. Modernizing a City Government. (Chicago: The Commission, 1954).

44. City Council of Portland, Oregon. The Portland Handbook. (Portland: The Council, 1969).

45. City-County Consolidation Steering Committee. Final Report: June 1971. (Sacramento, Ca.: The Committee, 1971).

46. City Income Taxes. (New York: The Tax Foundation, 1967).

47. Columbian Research Institute. Approaches to Local Government Reorganization, Tri-Cities, Washington. (Portland, Ore.: The Institute, March 1970).

48. ------. Financial Impact of Governmental Reorganization: Sacramento. (Portland, Ore.: The Institute, 1974).

49. ------. Fiscal Implications of Government Unification: Multnomah County. (Portland: The Institute, 1969).

     The consultant was hired by a Portland, Oregon local government study group to explore the fiscal impacts of city-county consolidation in the Portland area. While overly optomistic in many respects, the study projects the effects of unification in the Portland situation, and in part provided reinforcing support to the study group's continuing efforts to establish enabling legislation persuing consolidation as an alternative.

50. Columbus, Georgia, City of. Organization Chart for Columbus, Georgia Consolidated Government. (Columbus: The City, n.d.).

51. Committee for Economic Development. Reshaping Government in Metropolitan Areas. (New York: The Committee, 1970).

     One of the major national organizations that has endorsed the consolidation concept, the C.E.D. recommends unification as an alternative to the "crazy quilt" patchwork of governments found in most metropolitan areas.

52. Conference on Consolidated Government. The New City: 1968 and Beyond. (Jacksonville: The Conference, 1968).

53. Coomer, James C. Nashville-Davidson County: A Study of Metropolitan Government. (Chicago: American Political Science Association, 1969).

54. Cresap, McCormick and Paget, Inc. Improving Police Service in Suburban Cook County. (Chicago: Cresap, McCormick and Paget, Inc., 1971).

55. Dade County Manager's Office. A Status Report of Metropolitan Dade County, Florida. (Miami: County Manager, January 4, 1968).

56. ------. Facts and Figures, 1970-1971. (Miami: County Manager's Office, 1970).

57. ------. The Home Rule Amendment and Charter. (Miami: County Manager's Office, 1969).

58. Danielson, Michael N. (Ed.). Metropolitan Politics: A Reader. (Boston: Little, Brown and Company, 1966).

59. Dawson, Russell. Selected Factors Affecting Property Tax Revision for City-County Consolidation. (Portland: City-County Charter Commission, 1973).

    A consultant to the Portland Charter Commission, Dawson considers the economic costs to central city residents of commuters from suburban areas. He also analyzes techniques of equalizing service costs through differential taxation and user charges.

60. DeArnold, R.N. The Founding of Juneau. (Juneau: Gastineau Channel Centennial Association, 1967).

61. Denver Planning Office. Denver - 1969. (Denver: The Planning Office, 1969).

62. Department of Urban Studies, National League of Cities. Reorganizing Local Government for the Future: Staff Report 67-3. (Washington, D.C.: The League, 1967).

63. Division of Local Government. Problems of Local Government. (Denver: State of Colorado, 1968).

64. Douglas, Paul H. Building the American City: Report of the National Committee on Urban Problems to the Congress and to the President of the United States. (Washington, D.C.: U.S. Government Printing Office, 1968).

65. Dovell, J.E. City-County Consolidating: Its Possibilities in Florida. (Gainsville: University of Florida 1956).

66. Duncombe, Herbert S. County Government in America. (Washington, D.C.: National Association of Counties Research Foundation, 1966).

67. Durham Charter Commission. Report of the Durham City-County Charter Commission. (Durham, N.C.: The Commission, 1960).

68. Economic Research Service of the U.S. Department of Agriculture. Impact of City-County Consolidation of the Rural-Urban Fringe: Nashville-Davidson County, Tennessee, (Washington, D.C.: U.S. Government Printing Office, 1971).

   A federal government survey was made of the fringe area almost eight years after consolidation. In general, the survey found citizen satisfaction with the new government, and a fairly high degree of identification with the new "Metro" agency.

69. Education Committee of the Committee on Consolidation. Facts About Consolidation. (Winchester, Va.: The Committee, 1969).

70. Elazar, D.J. A Case of Failure in Attempted Metropolitan Integration: Nashville and Davidson County, Tennessee. (Chicago: National Opinion Research Center, 1961).

71. Etter, Orval. The Metropolitan Borough: What is It? (Portland: Portland Metropolitan Study Commission, 1966).

72. Goodall, Leonard E. The American Metropolis. (Columbus, Ohio: Charles E. Merrill Company, 1968). Pp. 97-112.

73. Goode, R. Ray. Legislative Program: Memorandum. (Miami: Dade County Manager's Office, October 20, 1970).

74. -----. 1971 Legislative Program. (Miami: Dade County Manager's Office, January 22, 1971).

75. "Governmental Data for Cities Over 5,000 Population," in Municipal Year Book. (Chicago: International City Managers' Association, 1963). Pp. 158-207.

76. Governmental Research Bureau (Park College). The County
       and Intergovernmental Relations. (Kansas City, Mo.:
       The College, 1968). P. 17.

77. Governmental Research Institute. County-City Consolida-
       tion. (Lincoln, Neb.: The Institute, 1972).

78. Grant, Daniel R. The States and the Urban Crisis.
       (Englewood Cliffs, N.J.: Prentice-Hall, 1969). Pp.
       68-80.

            Grant discusses the need for the states to
       take a more active role in encouraging metropolitan
       reorganizations. History has shown the states to
       be relatively passive, only occasionally encourag-
       ing even functional consolidation or the assumption
       by counties of municipal functions.

79. -----. "Political Access under Metropolitan Government:
       A Comparative Study of Perceptions by Knowledgables,"
       in Daland, R. (Ed.). Comparative Urban Research.
       (Beverly Hills: Sage, 1969). Pp. 249-271.

80. Hall, William. A Study of Transition Problems in the
       City of Portland and Multnomah County, Oregon.
       (Portland: City of Portland, 1974).

            Hall analyzes the proposed Portland-Multnomah
       County city-county charter's transition provisions,
       designed to blend the city, county and special
       districts into one governmental unit. He makes
       recommendations for administrative reorganization,
       personnel relations, and the obtaining of legal
       advice to facilitate an orderly change-over.

81. Harder, Bruce C. City-County Consolidation. (Vancouver,
       Wa.: Regional Planning Council of Clark County,
       1971).

            A brief study of consolidation implications
       for the Clark County, Washington area, this report
       concentrates on the provisions of Washington state
       law relating to consolidation and the implications
       for the planning function. It is one of the series
       of internship studies sponsored by the Western
       Intergovernmental Center for Higher Education.

82. Haupman, Jerzy (Ed.). The County and Intergovernmental
       Relations. (Parksville, Mo.: Park College Govern-
       mental Research Bureau, 1968).

83. Havard, William C. and Floyd L. Corty. <u>Rural-Urban</u>
    <u>Consolidation</u>. (Baton Rouge: Louisiana State
    University Press, 1964).

    This book represents the first major case
    study in book length of a consolidated city-county
    - Baton Rouge. The authors exhaustively examine
    consolidation's effects in the areas of planning,
    public works, and finances. The many tables in
    the appendix make this a particularly valuable
    quantitative addition to the consolidation litera-
    ture.

84. Hawkins, Brett W. <u>Nashville Metro: The Politics of City-</u>
    <u>County Consolidation</u>. (Nashville: Vanderbilt Uni-
    versity Press, 1966).

    An excellent case study of the Nashville
    consolidation. The "formative years" of 1951-1958
    are closely examined, as are the interim years of
    1958-1962. The last half of the book is devoted
    to the successful 1962 referenda, in particular a
    close examination of voting patterns and citizen
    attitudes toward the vote itself. The text is
    liberally supplemented with tables, which lend
    great clarity to the subject.

85. Hawley, Amos H. and Basil G. Zimmer. "Resistance to
    Unification in a Metropolitan Community," in
    Janowitz, Morris (Ed.). <u>Community Political</u>
    <u>Systems</u>. (Glencoe, Ill.: The Free Press, 1970).
    Pp. 170-182.

86. -----. <u>The Metropolitan Community</u>. (Beverly Hills: Sage
    1970).

    This survey of six cities finds "monumental"
    opposition to the consolidation concept. While
    half the sample had studied reorganization during
    the 1960's, none of the six cities have ever voted
    on the question of city-county consolidation. The
    authors also conclude that support for consolidatio
    increases with socio-economic status, but in no
    "appreciable numbers."

87. Healy, Patrick. "Municipal Government in 1962," in <u>Muni-</u>
    <u>cipal Year Book</u>. (Chicago: International City
    Managers' Association, 1963). Pp. 20-73.

88. Holloran, Jerry R. Local Government: Constitutional
    Convention Study No. 16. (Helena: Montana
    Constitutional Convention Commission, 1971).

89. Honolulu, City and County of. The City and County of
    Honolulu. (Honolulu: The City-County, May 1969).

90. House Committee on Government Operations. Government
    in Metropolitan Areas. (Washington, D.C.:
    Committee Print, 1961).

91. Howe, William M. "Municipal History of New Orleans," in
    Abrams, Herbert B. (Ed.). Johns Hopkins Univer-
    sity Studies in Historical and Political Science.
    (Baltimore: Johns Hopkins University Press, 1889).
    Pp. 159-187.

92. Housing and Urban Development, Department of. State
    Urban Information and Technical Assistance Services
    - The First Six Months. (Washington, D.C.: HUD
    Clearinghouse Service, 1969).

93. Institute of Public Administration. Partnership for
    Progress: Atlanta-Fulton County Consolidation.
    (New York: The Institute, 1970).

        A presentation of reorganization alternatives
    made to the Joint Atlanta-Fulton County Citizens
    Advisory Committee. The study outlines the histor-
    ical cooperation of the two governments, and
    provides evaluations of other metropolitan agencies.
    Despite this careful evaluation and presentation of
    alternatives, no vote was ever taken in the Atlanta
    area on the question of consolidation.

94. Interim Committee on Urban Affairs. Urban Affairs and
    Mass Transit. (Salem, Ore.: State of Oregon, 1970).

95. Jacksonville, City of. October 1, 1968: A Date with
    Destiny. (Jacksonville, Fla.: City of Jacksonville,
    1968).

96. -----. A Better Place to Live Each Year. (Jacksonville:
    The City, 1970).

97. Jerry, J. Michael. Jurisdictional Changes: Annexations
    and Consolidation: Report No. 1. (Madison, Wisc.:
    State of Wisconsin, 1970).

98. Jones, Victor. Metropolitan Government. (Chicago: Uni-
    versity of Chicago, 1942).

99. Kaplan, Harold. <u>Urban Political Systems: A Functional Analysis of Metro Toronto.</u> (New York: Columbia University Press, 1967).

100. Kean, R. Gordon Jr. <u>The Baton Rouge Plan,</u> (Baton Rouge, La.: The City, n.d.).

101. Kneier, Charles M. <u>City Government in the United States.</u> (New York: Harper and Brothers, 1957). Pp. 311-314.

102. Lawson, Bruce G. <u>Merger and Consolidation of Local Government Units in the State of Oregon.</u> (Eugene, Ore.: University of Oregon, 1969).

103. League of Oregon Cities. <u>Proposed Oregon Municipal Policy.</u> (Salem, Ore.: The League, 1970).

104. League of Virginia Counties. <u>Research Report No. 5: Statement Pertaining to Annexation, Consolidation, and the Structure of Local Government in Virginia.</u> (Charlottesville, Va: The League, 1963).

105. League of Women Voters. <u>Guide to Virginia Beach Government.</u> (Virginia Beach, Va.: The League, 1972).

106. ------. <u>Virginia Beach.</u> (Virginia Beach, Va,: The League, 1968).

107. League of Women Voters of Nevada. <u>Support of a Constitutional Amendment to Allow the Consolidation of Carson City and Ormsby County: State C.R. Background No. 2.</u> (Carson City, Nev.: The League, 1968).

108. Legislative Research Commission. <u>City-County Consolidation: Research Report No. 64.</u> (Frankfort, Ky.: The Commission, 1971).

109. Littlefield, Neil. <u>Metropolitan Area Problems and Municipal Home Rule.</u> (Ann Arbor: University of Michigan Law School, 1962).

110. Local Affairs Agency. <u>Borough and City Property and Sales Tax Rates.</u> (Juneau, Alas.: Governor's Office, 1971).

111. Local Government Study Commission. <u>Consolidation Charter: Ft. Pierce, St. Lucie County, Florida.</u> (Ft. Pierce, Fla.: The Commission, 1972).

112. Local Government Study Commission of Duval County. *Blueprint for Improvement.* (Jacksonville: The Commission, 1966).

113. Local Government Study Commission of Escambia, Florida. *Report of the Local Government Study Commission of Escambia County, Florida.* (Pensacola: The Commission, 1966).

114. Long, Norton E. *The Polity.* (Chicago: Rand, McNally and Company, 1962). P. 160.

115. Lybrand, Ross Brothers, and Montgomery (CPA). *Program for Combining Electronic Data Processing Systems.* (Portland, Ore.: Lybrand, Ross Brothers, and Montgomery, 1965).

116. Lyons, S.R. *Citizen Attitudes and Metropolitan Government.* (Charlotte, N.C.: Institute for Urban Studies and Community Service, University of North Carolina, 1972).

117. MacDonald, Austin F. *American City Government and Administration.* (New York: Thomas Y. Crowell Company, 1956).

118. Macy, William F. *The Story of Old Nantucket.* (Boston: Houghton Mifflin Company, 1928).

119. Maddox, Russell W. *Issues in State and Local Government: Selected Readings.* (Princeton, N.J.: D. Van Nostrand, 1965).

120. -----, and Robert F. Fuquay. *State and Local Government.* (Princeton, N.J.: D. Van Nostrand, 1962). Pp. 564-567.

121. Makielski, S.J. Jr. *City-County Consolidation: A Guide for Virginians.* (Charlottesville, Va.: Institute of Government, University of Virginia, 1971).

   A general guide to various charter aspects of Virginia consolidation agreements. Virginia charters are first designed by local commissions, approved by the state legislature, and are then submitted to the voters. This text analyzes the representational, financial, personnel, and service function aspects of Virginia's proposed consolidation charters. It also provides a guide to pre-campaign study and to campaign tactics.

122. -----. *Local Planning in Virginia: Development, Politics, and Prospects.* (Charlottesville, Va.: Institute of Government, University of Virginia, 1969).

123. Mariner, Elwyn E. *This is Your Massachusetts Government.* (Arlington Heights, Mass.: Mariner Books, 1970). Pp. 135-144.

124. Marion County Republican Central Committee. *Your Government: Blueprint for the Future.* (Indianapolis, Ind.: The Committee, 1970).

125. Martin, Richard. *Consolidation: Jacksonville-Duval County; The Dynamics of Urban Political Reform.* (Jacksonville: Convention Press, 1968).

Martin, a journalist in Jacksonville during the consolidation campaign, has compiled a history of the problems besetting Jacksonville prior to consolidation. The author writes from a subjective standpoint, due to his close connection with the actors and events - particularly the indictment of local officials for corruption and the disaccreditation of local schools. Overall, this book provides the most complete record of the Jacksonville consolidation campaign, and provides many insights into local government crises and campaign tactics.

126. -----. *A Summary of Consolidation: Jacksonville-Duval County; The Dynamics of Urban Political Reform.* (Jacksonville: Convention Press, 1968). Mimeo.

127. Martin, Roscoe C. *Metropolis in Transition.* (Washington, D.C.: Housing and Home Finance Agency, 1963). Pp. 103-114.

128. Massachusetts, State of. *News Release #JY-46.* (Boston: Governor's Press Office, July 10, 1970).

129. -----. *House No. 5453: Legislative Research Council Report Relative to Voluntary Muncipal Merger Procedures.* (Boston: Wright and Potter Printing Company, 1970).

130. -----. *House No. 4988: Legislative Research Council Report Relative to Regional Government.* (Boston: Wright and Potter Printing Company, 1970).

131. -----. House No. 6125: Report of the Special Commission
      Relative to the Modernization of County Government.
      (Boston: Wright and Potter Printing Company, 1970).

132. McElliott, Michael. Summation of Historical Development
      of City-County Consolidation Efforts in Portland/
      Multnomah, With Illustrated Material on Consolida-
      tion Efforts Elsewhere. (Portland, Ore.: Portland
      Metropolitan Study Commission, 1966). Mimeo.

133. -----. Efficiency and Responsibility Through Two-Tier
      Metropolitan Government. (Portland, Ore.: Portland
      Metropolitan Study Commission, 1968). Mimeo.

134. McLean, Joseph A. Annual Report of the City and Borough
      of Juneau, Alaska, July 1, 1970-June 30, 1971.
      (Juneau: City and Borough of Juneau, 1971).

135. Memphis and Shelby County Charter Commission. Charter
      of the Consolidated Government of Memphis and
      Shelby County. (Memphis: The Commission, 1962).

136. Merger Information Center Committee. Questions and
      Answers about the Proposed Merger of Local Govern-
      ment. (Macon, Ga.: The Committee, 1960).

137. Metropolitan Government Charter Commission. Proposed
      Charter of the Metropolitan Government of Nashville
      and Davidson County, Tennessee. (Nashville: The
      Commission, 1962).

138. Municipal Consolidation in the Jackson Community. (Lan-
      sing, Mich.: Citizen's Research Council of Michigan,
      1966).

139. Murphy, Thomas P. Metropolitics and the Urban County.
      (Washington, D.C.: Washington National Press, 1970).

140. Nansemond, City of. Budget: City of Nansemond, Virginia
      and its Predecessors. (Nansemond, Va.: The City,
      1972).

141. Nashville and Davidson County Planning Commissions.
      Organization of the Office of Metropolitan County
      Mayor. (Nashville: The Commissions, 1963).

142. National Association of Counties. Consolidation: Partial
      or Total? (Washington, D.C.: NACO, 1973).

65

The text is a partial transcript of NACO's
fourth consolidation conference, held in Jacksonville in February of 1973. While no conclusions
are reached, some thorough discussions are
presented on the progress of the consolidated
governments of Jacksonville, Indianapolis, Baton
Rouge, Nashville, and Lexington.

143. -----. Guide to County Organization and Management.
(Washington, D.C.: NACO, 1968).

144. -----. Proceedings of the Urban County Congress.
(Washington, D.C.: NACO, 1959).

145. National League of Cities. Adjusting Municipal Boundaries: Law and Practice. (Washington, D.C.: Department of Urban Studies, The League, 1966).

146. Nelson, Howard J. A Case Study of Failure in Attempted
Metropolitan Integration: Nashville and Davidson
County. (Chicago: University of Chicago, 1961).

147. New Jersey, State of. Joint Services - A Response to
Area-Wide Problems. (Trenton, N.J.: County and
Municipal Government Study Commission, 1970).

148. -----. Creative Localism - A Prospectus. (Trenton,
N.J.: County and Municipal Government Study Commission, 1968).

149. -----. County Government - Challenge and Change.
(Trenton, N.J.: County and Municipal Government
Study Commission, 1969).

150. North Dakota, Legislative Council of. State, Federal,
and Local Government. (Bismark, N.D.: State of
North Dakota, 1970).

151. Norton, James A. The Metro Experience. (Cleveland,
Ohio: The Press of Case Western Reserve University,
1963).

152. Ohio Department of Urban Affairs. Councils of Government. (Columbus, Ohio: State of Ohio, October
1969).

153. Paglin, Morton. The Economics of Metropolitan Consolidation. (Portland, Ore.: Portland State University,
1967).

A study prepared for the Portland Metropolitan

Study Commission, this economic analysis reflects
negatively on the "economies-of-scale" arguments
used by proponents of consolidation. Paglin
argues that such economies can only be realized
up to certain population sizes, and that beyond
those levels increased size means increased cost
per unit. However, the bulk of his arguments
are based on studies of St. Louis, a city separated
from its county for a century.

154. Pennsylvania, State of. Setting the Focus. (Philadel-
      phia: Pennsylvania Economic League (Eastern Divi-
      sion), September 1963).

155. Philadelphia, City of. Organization of Philadelphia's
      City Government. (Philadelphia: The City, Septem-
      ber 1970).

156. Pock, Max A. Consolidating Police Functions in Metro-
      politan Areas. (Ann Arbor, Mich.: University of
      Michigan Law School, 1962).

157. Podell, Bertram L. Proposal: Local Government Consolida-
      tion -- A Means to Greater Economy and Efficiency
      in New York. (Albany, N.Y.: New York State Assem-
      bly, 1967).

158. Portland Metropolitan Study Commission. Memorandum:
      Regional Planning: An End of Too Little, Too Late.
      (Portland, Ore.: The Commission, 1966).

159. -----. Report and Recommendations of the Portland
      Metropolitan Study Commission: 1971. (Portland,
      Ore.: The Commission, 1971).

160. -----. Memorandum: The Consolidation of Nashville and
      Davidson County. (Portland, Ore.: The Commission,
      1967).

161. -----. Memorandum: Paradise Lost? (Portland, Ore.:
      The Commission, 1967).

162. -----. City-County Consolidation. (Portland, Ore.:
      The Commission, 1969).

163. -----. Memorandum: Will Consolidation Work? Reshaping
      Local Government. (Portland, Ore.: The Commission,
      1969).

164. -----. Constitutionality of 'Differential Taxation' as
      Provided for in House Bill 1054. (Portland, Ore.:
      The Commission, 1971).

165. ------. A Charter Establishing the Municipality of
      Greater Portland and Providing for the Establish-
      ment of Corporate Communities Therein (Preliminary
      Draft. (Portland, Ore.: The Commission, 1967).

166. ------. Memorandum: City-County Consolidation in
      Jacksonville and Duval County, Florida. (Portland,
      Ore.: The Commission, October 25, 1967).

167. Public Administration Service. State and Local Govern-
      ment Relationships in the State of Hawaii. (Chi-
      cago: Public Administration Service, 1962).

168. Report to the Legislature, 1961 Session, by the Senate
      Fact-Finding Committee on Local Government.
      (Sacramento, Ca.: State of California, 1961).

169. Rhodes, Donald G. The Baton Rouge City-Parish Consoli-
      dation: A History and Evaluation. (Baton Rouge:
      Louisiana State University Unpublished Master's
      Thesis, 1956).

170. Richardson, Richard J. Orleans Parish Offices: Notes
      on City-Parish Consolidation. (New Orleans:
      Bureau of Governmental Research, 1961).

171. Rogers, David. The Management of Big Cities. (Beverly
      Hills: Sage, 1971).

           Rogers briefly discusses the Philadelphia
      city institutional changes of the period 1948-1960,
      following Philadelphia's adoption of a consolida-
      tion charter under home rule status. He concentra-
      tes more on the strategies and approaches of the
      consolidated government to problems of civil
      rights, housing, and economic development than
      administrative or legal consequences of the charter
      adoption.

172. Rush, John A. The City-County Consolidated. (Los
      Angeles: By the Author, 1941).

           A member of the Denver Charter Convention of
      1898, Rush compiled the first comprehensive study
      of the "city-county consolidated." He has lumped
      all city-counties under the category of consolida-
      tions, including St. Louis, Baltimore, and the
      independent cities of Virginia. This text provides
      insights into the legislative-mandated consolida-
      tions, and provides first-hand data on the
      political manuverings behind the Denver merger.

173. Rutledge, Hugh. All Systems "Go" for UNIGOV January 1. (Indianapolis: Mayor's Office, October 18, 1969). Press Release.

174. ------. Making UNIGOV Work. (Indianapolis: Mayor's Office, May 12-19, 1969). Series of five press releases.

175. San Francisco, City and County of. City and County of San Francisco. (San Francisco: The City, 1971).

176. ------. San Francisco Statistical Data. (San Francisco: The City, 1970).

177. ------. Information Sheet, San Francisco, California. (San Francisco: The City, 1970).

178. ------. The Consolidated City and County Government of San Francisco. (San Francisco: The City, 1966).

179. ------. Board of Supervisors: City and County of San Francisco. (San Francisco: The City, 1970).

180. ------. Summary of the Charter of the City and County of San Francisco. (San Francisco: The City, n.d.).

181. Sayre, Wallace S. and Herman Kaufman. Governing New York City. (New York: Russell Sage Foundation, 1961).

   A text considered to be the definitive work on New York City government. The first chapter details the history and personalities involved in the creation of "Greater New York City," including politics involved at the state level. A facinating story well told, although the economic, political and legal ramifications of the consolidation itself are not discussed.

182. Schmandt, Henry J., Paul G. Steinbicker, and George D. Wendell. Metropolitan Reform in St. Louis: A Case Study. (New York: Holt, Rinehart and Winston, 1961).

183. Schmandt, Henry J. and William Standing. The Milwaukee Metropolitan Study Commission. (Bloomington, Ind.: Indiana University Press, 1965).

184. Sengstock, Frank S. Consolidation: Building A Bridge Between City and Suburb. (Worchester: Hefferman Press, 1964).

185. Simon, Herbert A. Fiscal Aspects of Urban Consolidation
(Berkeley: University of California, 1943).

186. Sitka, City and Borough of. Budget of the City and
Borough of Sitka, 1972-1973. (Stika: The City,
1972).

187. Snow, C. Why Consolidate Macon and Bibb County Governments? (Macon, Ga.: The Author, 1960).

188. Sofen, Edward. The Miami Metropolitan Experiment. (New
York: Doubleday-Anchor, 1966).

189. South Dakota, State of. South Dakota Planning and
Development Districts. (Sioux Falls: The State,
n.d.).

190. -----. Revised Planning Legislation, House Bill 846.
(Sioux Falls: The State, February 17, 1970).

191. State Legislative Affairs Agency. City-Borough Unification Proposals: A Preliminary Look at the
Question. (Juneau, Alas.: The Agency, 1967).

192. Taxpayers for Consolidated Government. Break the Chain
of Waste and Duplication. (Chattanooga, Tenn.:
Taxpayers for Consolidated Government, 1970).

193. Tax Supervision and Conservation Commission. Cost
Comparison. (Portland, Ore.: The Commission, 1971).

194. Temple, David Graham. Merger Politics: Local Government Consolidation in Tidewater Virginia. (Charlottesville: University of Virginia, 1972).

195. -----. The Tidewater Mergers: The Politics of City-
County Consolidations in Virginia. (Charlottes-
ville: University of Virginia Unpublished Master's
Thesis, 1966).

196. Texas, State of. Texas Urban Community Development Fact
Sheet. (Austin: The State, n.d.).

197. UNESCO. Handbook for Social Research in Urban Areas.
(Paris: UN Publishing, 1964).

198. Urban Action Clearinghouse, U.S. Chamber of Commerce.
Jacksonville, Florida Merges City and County
Governments: Case Study No. 4. (Washington, D.C.:
U.S. Chamber of Commerce, 1968).

The Clearinghouse has prepared a brief (20
pages), simplified case study of the situation
surrounding the Jacksonville-Duval consolidation
campaign. Only four pages are devoted to textual
development, but the tables and documents in the
remainder are valuable in determining the progres-
sion of the consolidation from concept to consuma-
tion.

199. -----. City-County Consolidation: Columbus, Georgia:
Case Study No. 18. (Washington, D.C.: Chamber of
Commerce of the United States, 1971).

Another brief case study of consolidation,
with supporting documents including excerpts from
the enabling legislation and newspaper articles
clipped during the campaign.

200. Urban Studies Center, Portland State University.
Annexation, Incorporation and Consolidation in
the Portland Metropolitan Area. (Portland, Ore:
Portland State University, 1968).

201. -----. A Review of City/County/Special District Functional Relationships in the Portland Urban Area.
(Portland, Ore.: Portland State University, 1969).

202. Vance, Rupert B. and Sara Smith. "Metropolitan Dominance and Integration," in Cities in Society. (New
York: The Free Press, 1957).

203. Virginia Metropolitan Areas Study Commission. Governing
the Virginia Metropolitan Areas: An Assessment.
(Richmond, Va.: The Commission, 1967).

204. Warner, Sam B. Jr. The Private City. (Philadelphia:
University of Pennsylvania Press, 1968).

Seven pages are devoted to the historical
development of the 1854 consolidation of Philadelphia and Philadelphia County. The pressures of
Abolition, race riots, police corruption, and state-
local power struggles are analyzed in their effect
on the consolidation movement. Unfortunately,
Philadelphia proved the point that governmental
reform cannot succeed in an environment of "weakness
and corruption."

71

205. Warren, Robert O. _Government in Metropolitan Regions: A Reappraisal of Fractionated Political Organizations._ (Davis, Ca.: University of California Institute of Governmental Affairs, 1966).

206. Washington State Research Council. _City-County Consolidation: A Study of Its Possibilities for Walla-Walla, Washington._ (Olympia, Wa.: The Council, January 1967).

207. Washington State University Bureau of Government Research. _Proposed City-County Consolidation Constitutional Amendment._ (Seattle: Washington State University, n.d.).

208. White, Anthony G. _A Regional Approach: City-County Consolidation as a Method of Local Governmental Reorganization._ (Portland, Ore.: Portland State University Unpublished Master's Thesis, 1971).

209. -----. _A Selected Bibliography: City-County Consolidation in the United States._ (Monticello, Ill.: Council of Planning Librarians, 1972). Exchange Bibliography No. 294.

210. Wicker, Warren J. _Consolidation: An Account of the Activities Surrounding the Effort to Consolidate the City of Charlotte and Mecklenberg County, North Carolina, March 1971._ (Chapel Hill, N.C.: University of North Carolina at Chapel Hill, 1971).

211. Williams, Oliver P. _Metropolitan Political Analysis: A Social Access Approach._ (New York: The Free Press, 1971). Pp. 81-84.

212. Williamsburg-James City County Joint Consolidation Study Commission. _Report of the Williamsburg-James City County Joint Consolidation Study Commission._ (Williamsburg, Va.: The Commission, 1963).

213. Willmont, John F. "City-County Consolidation," in _Notes and References._ Volume 4. (New York: Governmental Research Association, 1948).

214. -----. _The Truth About City-County Consolidation._ (Miami: Dade County Research Foundation, 1948).

215. Winchester, City of. _Annexation Information._ (Winchester, Va.: The City, 1970).

216. Wisconsin, State of. Alternative Approaches to Metropolitan Problems. (Madison, Wisc.: The State, n.d.).

217. Women Voters, League of. City-County Consolidation. (Portland, Ore.: Portland League of Women Voters, 1970).

218. Zimmerman, Joseph F. Metropolitan Charters. (Albany, N.Y.: State University of New York, 1967).

    To make available sample charters to metropolitan areas considering reform, Zimmerman has collected and printed the charters of Baton Rouge, Nashville-Davidson County, Metropolitan Dade County, Toronto, London (England), the Port of New York Authority, and the Metropolitan Seattle Sewage District. Each document is introduced by a brief history of its adoption.

219. -----. Government and the Metropolis: Selected Readings. (New York: Holt, Rinehart and Winston, 1968).

220. -----. "Local Government and Metropolitan Area Developments in 1969," in Municipal Year Book. (Chicago: International City Managers' Association, 1970).

II. Periodicals; Major News Articles

221. "ACIR Recommends 'Drastic' Changes to Solve Urban
        Problems," Metropolitan Area Digest. Vol. XIII,
        No. 1, January-February 1970, p. 7.

222. Anderson, W.G. Jr. "Charleston County Voters Defeat
        Consolidation Plan," National Civic Review. Vol.
        63, No. 11, December 1974, p. 592.

223. "Annexations, Mergers Draw Interest," Nations Cities.
        December 1969.

224. "Atlanta Area Considers City-County Merger," Metropoli-
        tan Area Digest. Vol. XI, No. 1, January-February
        1968, p. 5.

225. Auble, Phillip M. "Major Issues Affecting City Govern-
        ment in 1971," Western City. April 1971.

226. Banfield, Edward C. "The Politics of Metropolitan Area
        Organization," Midwest Journal of Political Science.
        Vol. 1, No. 1, May 1957.

227. "Baton Rouge City-County Plan Submitted," National Civic
        Review. Vol. XXXVI, No. 7, July 1947.

228. "Baton Rouge Votes Consolidation," National Civic Review.
        Vol. XXXVI, No. 9, September 1947, pp. 468-469.

229. Beckman, R. "Alternate Approaches for Metropolitan
        Reorganization," Public Management. Vol. XLVI, No.
        5, May 1964.

230. Bowen, John. "The Newport News-Warwick Merger," The
        Commonwealth. Vol. XXV, August 1958, pp. 27-29.

231. Braestrup, Peter. "Indianapolis Suburbanites Find
        Cause to Cheer Merger," The Washington Post.
        September 8, 1970.

232. Brown, R.M. "The Urban Crisis," Greater Portland
        Commerce. Vol. 52, No. 36, September 1966.

233. Burgess, James V. "Consolidation in Georgia: Columbus
        and Muscogee County Merge Governments January 1,"
        Nation's Cities. December 1970.

234. Burke, D. Barlow. "Courts and City-County Consolidation in Philadelphia," _Dickinson Law Review_. Vol. 57, 1952, pp. 24-30.

   Burke discusses the implications of the 1951 Pennsylvania constitutional amendment to allow consolidation with respect to Philadelphian courts. This article was written soon after the "reconsolidation" and home-rule charter adoption in Philadelphia, and the author admits that the article is premature in the consideration of all implications of court consolidation provisions in the new charter.

235. Caile, Charlene. "Bringing the City and County Together," _The American County_. February 1972, pp. 8-19.

236. ------. "Recipe for Better Local Government," _County News/New County Times_. Vol. 2, No. 1, February 1973.

237. Campbell, Don. "'UNIGOV' in Indianapolis," _Hartford_ (Connecticut) _Times_. February 10, 1970.

238. Carver, Joan. "Responsiveness and Consolidation," _Urban Affairs Quarterly_. Vol. 9, No. 2, December 1973, pp. 211-250.

   Ms. Carver, a political scientist from Jacksonville University, concludes from her study that the Jacksonville consolidation has gained the support of a broad spectrum of socioeconomic classes, although the low-income white residents exhibit little involvement. She also concludes that metropolitan governments with greater problem-solving capabilities may not utilize their resources fully to attack social problems and involve citizens in their governments.

239. Cassella, William N. Jr. "Merger Proposed in Albuquerque," _National Civic Review_. Vol. XLVII, No. 3, March 1968, pp. 125-127.

240. "Chance for Nashville-Davidson County Metro," _Metropolitan Area Problems News and Digest_. Vol. IV, No. 5, September-October 1961, p. 7.

241. "Chattanooga Area Defeats Charter," _National Civic Review_. Vol. LIX, No. 11, December 1970, pp. 595-596.

242. "Chattanooga Considers City-County Charter," National Civic Review. Vol. LII, No. 6, June 1963, p. 502.

243. "City and County Plan School Consolidation," Metropolitan Area Problems News and Digest. Vol. VI, No. 4, July-August 1963, p. 1.

244. "City-County Agency Proposed to Promote Syracuse Growth," Metropolitan Area Problems News and Digest. Vol. VI, No. 3, May-June 1963, p. 7.

245. "City-County Commission Proposes Single Government," National Civic Review. Vol. 61, No. 6, June 1972, p. 361.

246. "City-County Consolidation: '70's Trend?" Nation's Cities. November 1969.

247. "City-County Consolidations," National Civic Review. Vol. 61, No. 1, January 1972, p. 37.

248. "City of Knoxville and Knox County Consolidate Libraries," Metropolitan Area Digest. Vol. X, No. 6, November-December 1967, p. 5.

249. "City Size Jumps; New Brunswick Abolishes County Government," Public Management. Vol. XLIX, No. 7, July 1967, p. 204.

250. "Clinton County to Build City-County Jail," Metropolitan Area Digest. Vol. XI, No. 4, September-October 1968, p. 4.

251. Cole, R.L. and David A. Caputo. "Leadership Opposition to Consolidation," Urban Affairs Quarterly. Vol. 8, No. 2, December 1972, pp. 253-258.

252. "Columbus, Muscogee County Merge in Georgia," Metropolitan Area Digest. Vol. XIII, No. 4, July-August 1970, p. 7.

253. "Committee for Economic Development Recommends Drastic Reduction in Number of Local Governments," Metropolitan Area Digest. Vol. IX, No. 5, September-October 1966, p. 1.

254. Condon, George A. "City-County Merger Sought in Knoxville," National Civic Review. Vol. XLVII, No. 12, December 1958, pp. 572-573.

255. "Consolidated Government Meets Urban-Rural Needs," Metro-
     politan Area Problems News and Digest. Vol. VI,
     No. 3, May-June 1963, p. 2.

256. "Consolidated Services Topic of National Conference in
     Florida," County News/New County Times. Vol. 1,
     No. 9, December 15, 1972, p. 6.

257. "Consolidation Charter Proposed for Charleston,"
     National Civic Review. Vol. 61, No. 5, May 1972,
     p. 255.

258. "Consolidation Move in Tennessee," Metropolitan Area
     Problems News and Digest. Vol. V, No. 1,
     January-February 1962, p. 8.

259. "Consolidation of Services Advised in Indiana," Metro-
     politan Area Problems News and Digest. Vol. III,
     No. 6, November-December 1960, p. 2.

260. "Consolidation Succeeds in Indiana, Fails in New Jersey,
     Pending in Oregon," Metropolitan Area Digest. Vol.
     XII, No. 3, May-June 1969, p. 6.

261. Cooper, Weldon. "The Charter and Virginia Local Govern-
     ment," University of Virginia News Letter. Vol.
     45, No. 8, April 15, 1969.

262. "County Consolidation Considered in Three Southeastern
     States," Metropolitan Area Digest. Vol. XII, No.
     2, March-April 1969, p. 1.

263. "County News Roundup," National Civic Review. Vol. 61,
     No. 1, January 1972, p. 36.

264. "County-Wide Liquor Stores? To Keep the Door Closed,
     Reject Metro," The Nashville Banner. June 27,
     1962.

265. "Countywide Unit Proposed in Florida," National Civic
     Review. Vol. LVI, No. 4, April 1967, pp. 220-221.

266. Danahy, Paul W. Jr. "Local Government for Florida's
     Metropolitan Areas," Florida Bar Journal. Vol.
     XL, No. 1, January 1966, pp. 16-25.

267. "Davidson County Voters Defeat Consolidation Move,"
     Metropolitan Area Problems News and Digest. Vol.
     I, No. 5, June-July 1958, p. 1.

268. Davies, David. "Financing Urban Functions and Services,
      Law and Contemporary Problems. Vol. XXX, No. 1,
      Winter 1965.

269. "Defeat in Georgia," National Civic Review. Vol. 63,
      No. 9, October 1974, p. 491.

270. DeWeese, R.W. "Policies of the Portland Chamber of
      Commerce," Greater Portland Commerce. Vol. 53,
      No. 5, February 1969.

271. Dixon, Robert G. Jr. "New Constitutional Forms for
      Metropolis: Reapportioned County Boards; Local
      Councils of Government," Law and Contemporary
      Problems. Vol. XXX, No. 1, Winter 1965.

272. -----. "Rebuilding the Urban Political System," George-
      town Law Review. Vol. LVIII, 1970, pp. 955-986.

273. "Durham Charter Commission Created," Metropolitan Area
      Problems News and Digest. Vol. II, No. 6, November-
      December 1959, p. 2.

274. "Durham Unified Charter Defeated," National Civic Review
      Vol. L, No. 3, March 1961, pp. 152, 170.

275. "Durham Voters Defeat Consolidation," Metropolitan Area
      Problems News and Digest. Vol. IV, No. 1,
      January-February 1961, p. 7.

276. "Duval County Voters Approve Partial Consolidation in
      the Jacksonville Area," Metropolitan Area Digest.
      Vol. X, No. 6, November-December 1967, p. 1.

277. Esser, George H. Jr. "Durham City-County Study Begun,"
      National Civic Review. Vol. XLVIII, No. 12,
      December 1959, pp. 586-587.

278. Etter, Orval. "Municipal Tax Differentials," Oregon Law
      Review. Vol. XXXVII, No. 1, December 1957.

            An extensive review of the state of different
      taxation in 1957. The tool of levying taxes at
      different rates according to services provided is
      used effectively by consolidated city-counties as
      a transition device.

279. -----. "Study Commission Ended in Portland," National
      Civic Review. Vol. LX, No. 9, September 1971, pp.
      458-460.

280. Farnsworth, E. Allan. "Problems of Local Governments: Developments of the Recent Past," The Urban Lawyer. Vol. I, No. 1, Spring 1969, pp. 47-58.

281. Feldman, Mark B. and Everett L. Jassy. "Metropolitan County Government," Harvard Law Review. Vol. III, No. 3, 1960, pp. 526+.

       The authors argue that, in single-county SMSA's, the county is the "appropriate repository" for the transfer of municipal functions under functional consolidation. They discuss Dade, county home rule, contractual agreements, and other methods of providing services on a county/metropolitan area-wide basis.

282. Fillebrown, T. Scott. "The Nashville Story," National Civic Review. Vol. LVIII, No. 5, May 1969, pp. 197-200, 210.

283. "Fiscal Impact Studied for Sacramento County," National Civic Review. Vol. 63, No. 8, September 1974, pp. 433-434.

284. Garcia, F.C., P.L. Hain, and J. Conway. "Bernalillo County Voters Defeat Consolidation," National Civic Review. Vol. 63, No. 1, January 1974, pp. 32-34.

285. "Georgia Commission Group Establishes County Priorities," National Civic Review. Vol. 61, No. 1, January 1972, p. 36.

286. Glauberman, Zale. "County Home Rule: An Urban Necessity," The Urban Lawyer. Vol. 1, No. 2, September 1969, pp. 170-188.

287. Grand, Ann. "City-County Consolidation Under Study," The Oregon Freemason. Vol. 49, No. 10, March 1972, p. 20.

288. Grant, Daniel R. "A Comparison of Predictions and Experience with Nashville 'Metro'," Urban Affairs Quarterly. Vol. I, No. 1, September 1965, pp. 38-54.

289. -----. "An Early Appraisal of Metropolitan Government for Nashville and Davidson County," Atlantic Economic Review. Vol. XVII, No. 10, June 1967.

290. -----. "Consolidations Compared," National Civic Review. Vol. LII, No. 1, January 1963, pp. 10-29.

291. -----. "Government for Metropolis: A Nashville-Davidson County Proposal," Tennessee News Letter. Vol. XXXVII, April 1958, pp. 1-8.

292. -----. "Nashville Metro Charter Proposed," National Civic Review. Vol. XLVII, No. 5, May 1958, pp. 235-236.

293. -----. "Suburban Vote Downs Nashville Metro Charter," National Civic Review. Vol. XLVII, No. 9, September 1958, pp. 399-401.

294. -----. "Trends in Urban Government and Administration," Law and Contemporary Problems. Vol. XXX, No. 1, Winter 1965.

295. -----. "Urban and Suburban Nashville: A Case Study in Metropolitanism," Journal of Politics. February 1955, pp. 82-99.

296. -----, and Lee S. Greene. "Surveys, Dust, Action," National Civic Review. Vol. L, No. 10, October 1961, p. 466.

297. Hardy, James A. "Metropolitan Organization," Utah Law Review. Vol. X, 1966, pp. 517-541.

298. Harpster, James E. "Memphis Area Votes on Merger," National Civic Review. Vol. LI, No. 11, November 1962, pp. 570-572.

299. Hauson, Royce. "Toward a New Urban Democracy: Metropolitan Consolidation and Decentralization," Georgetown Law Review. Vol. LVIII, 1970, pp. 863-899.

300. Hawkins, Brett W. "Fringe-City Life-Style Distance and Fringe Support of Political Integration," American Journal of Sociology. Vol. 74, November 1968, pp. 248-255.

301. -----. "Life-Style, Demographic Distance and Voter Support of City-County Consolidation," Southwest Social Science Quarterly. Vol. 48, No. 4, December 1967, pp. 325-337.

    Hawkins examines several variables in relation to support of city-county consolidation proposals in several referenda, in both central city and

fringe areas. He finds that social rank and
familism are weakly positive in correlation with
"yes" central-city votes. In the fringe areas,
social rank correlates positively (but again
weakly) to "yes" votes, and no relationship
exists for familism. As social differences
increasingly favor the fringe area, the level of
support correspondingly increases.

302. -----. "Public Opinion and Metropolitan Reorganization
in Nashville," Journal of Politics. Vol. 28,
No. 2, May 1966, pp. 408-418.

303. Hays, Samuel P. "The Politics of Reform in Municipal
Government in the Progressive Era," Pacific North-
west Quarterly. Vol. 55, No. 4, October 1964, pp.
157-169.

304. Hester, L.A. "The Jacksonville Story," National Civic
Review. Vol. LIX, No. 2, February 1970, pp. 76-95.

305. Hill, R. Steven and William P. Maxam. "UNIGOV: The
First Year," National Civic Review. Vol. LX, No.
6, June 1971, pp. 310-314.

306. Hirsch, Werner Z. "Expenditure Implications of Metropolitan Growth and Consolidation," Review of
Economics and Statistics. August 1959.

307. Hobart, Lawrence. "Urban Government Debated," Public
Power. Vol. XXVI, November 1967, pp. 592-595.

308. Holden, Matthew Jr. "The Governance of the Metropolis
as a Problem in Diplomacy," Journal of Politics.
Vol. XXVI, August 1964, pp. 627-647.

309. "HUD Official Calls for Local Government Modernization,"
Metropolitan Area Digest. Vol. X, No. 6, November-
December 1967, p. 7.

310. Highes, James H. Jr. "Consolidated Government Suits Both
Rural and Urban Interest," County Officer. Vol.
XXIV, No. 8, April 1963, pp. 148-149.

311. Huston, Michael J. "Recent Developments in Indiana Law,"
Indiana Law Review. Vol. XLVII, No. 1, Fall 1971,
pp. 101-117.

Huston explores the constitutionality of the
UNIGOV's failure to consolidate all governmental
functions and services and thereby become uniform.

He sees problems in the implementation of the
differential tax and service district scheme,
particularly in the selection of representatives
from those districts. Huston concludes that there
is a representational problem, and suggests
potential solutions to head off legal action.

312. "Indianapolis Mayor Discusses 'UNIGOV'," National
        Civic Review. Vol. LIX, No. 1, January 1970.

313. "Intergovernmental-Contractual Relationships in Washing-
        ton," Western Cities. April 1969.

314. "Intergovernmental Cooperation - Key to the Future,"
        Kansas Government Journal. Vol. 54, No. 4, April
        1968.

315. "Jacksonville and Duval County, Florida to Merge,"
        Nation's Cities. September 1967, p. 30.

316. "Jacksonville and Duval County Unite," National Civic
        Review. Vol. LVI, No. 10, October 1967, pp. 532-
        535.

317. "Jacksonville holds "Largest City" Title Following
        Merger," Nation's Cities. November 1968, p. 27.

318. "Jacksonvillians Like Consolidated City Government,"
        The American City. April 1970.

319. Joachin, L.H. "Dollars Speak in City and County Consoli
        dation," The American City. Vol. 23, December 1920
        p. 639.

320. Jones, Victor. "The Organization of a Metropolitan
        Region." University of Pennsylvania Law Review.
        Vol. MV, 1957, pp. 538-541.

321. "Juneau, Douglas, Greater Juneau Borough Consolidate in
        Alaska," Metropolitan Area Digest. Vol. XII, No.
        4, July-August 1970, p. 7.

322. Kean, R. Gordon Jr. "Consolidation That Works," Nation
        Civic Review. Vol. XLV, No. 11, November 1956, pp.
        478-493.

323. Keane, Mark E. "The Necessity for Better Management in
        Local Government," The Urban Lawyer. Vol. II, No.
        2, Summer 1970, pp. 235-243.

324. Kelly, Marion M. "Albuquerque Votes Against Merger,"
     National Civic Review. Vol. XLVIII, No. 11,
     November 1959, pp. 533-534.

325. Kessel, John H. "Governmental Structure and Political
     Environment: A Statistical Note about American
     Cities," American Political Science Review. Vol.
     LVI, No. 3, September 1962, pp. 615-620.

326. Kirby, James C. Jr. "Constitutional Law - 1962 Tennessee
     Survey: Delegation of Legislative Power to Metropol-
     itan Charter Commission," Vanderbilt Law Review.
     Vol. XVI, 1963, pp. 649-655.

327. "Knoxville Vote Date Set," Metropolitan Area Problems
     News and Digest. Vol. II, No. 1, January-February
     1959, p. 7.

328. Lawrence, David M. and H. Rutherford Turnbull III.
     "UNIGOV: City-County Consolidation in Indianapolis,"
     Popular Government. November 1969, pp. 18-26.

         An analysis of the events leading up to the
     creation of the Indianapolis-Marion County UNIGOV.
     The authors concentrate on the roles of key
     personalities, particularly that of Mayor Lugar.

329. "League of Arizona Cities and Towns Examines Intergovern-
     mental Relations," Western Cities. July 1969.

330. "Legal Aspects of City-County Consolidation in Tennessee,"
     Tennessee Law Review. Vol. XXX, 1963, pp. 449-516.

331. Leiken, Lawrence S. "Governmental Schemes for the
     Metropolis and the Implementation of Metropolitan
     Change," Journal of Urban Law. Vol. 49, 1971, pp.
     667-687.

         This article presents an overview of various
     types of metropolitan reorganization. Leiken
     discusses not only the Nashville consolidation, but
     also discusses in some detail the Miami-Dade County
     plan.   He suggests that one possible answer to
     voter resistence to metropolitan reform would be
     for the federal government, in the manner of the
     British Parliament, to initiate and advocate
     metropolitan reorganization plans.

332. Lewis, Thomas P., James S. Kostas, and Charles N. Carres.
     "Consolidation - Complete or Functional - of City
     and County Governments in Kentucky," Kentucky Law
     Journal. Vol. XLII, No. 3, March 1954, pp. 295-333.

333. "Lexington-Fayette County Approve Merger Charter,"
      National Civic Review. Vol. 61, No. 11, December
      1972, p. 567.

334. "Lexington-Fayette Group Nears Charter Completion,"
      National Civic Review. Vol. 61, No. 6, June 1972,
      pp. 305-306.

335. Lineberry, Robert L. "Reforming Metropolitan Govern-
      ance: Requiem or Reality?" Georgetown Law Review.
      Vol. LVIII, 1970, pp. 675-717.

336. "Little Rock Studies Consolidation," Metropolitan Area
      Problems News and Digest. Vol. V, No. 3, May-June
      1962, p. 2.

337. "Louisville and Albuquerque Seek Annexation, Consolida-
      tion," Metropolitan Area Problems News and Digest.
      Vol. I, No. 3, February-March 1958, p. 5.

338. Lyons, W.E. and R.L. Engstrom. "Life-Style and Fringe
      Attitudes Toward the Political Integration of
      Urban Governments," Midwest Journal of Political
      Science. Vol. 15, August 1971, pp. 475-494.

339. Makielski, S.J. Jr. "City-County Consolidation in the
      U.S.," University of Virginia News Letter.
      October 15, 1969.

340. -----. "City-County Consolidation," Virginia Town and
      City. No. 4, July 1969, pp. 19-20.

341. Mayo, Fesler. "Denver Consolidation - A Shining Light,"
      National Municipal Review. No. 29, June 1940, p.
      380.

342. McDill, E.L. and J.C. Ridley. "Status, Anomia, Politi-
      cal Alienation, and Political Participation,"
      American Journal of Sociology. September 1962,
      pp. 205-213.

            An analysis of the first Nashville-Davidson
      County consolidation attempt, from a sociological
      standpoint. The authors conclude that the
      electorate was in a status of alienation and
      anomia with respect to their governments in 1958,
      and would not have adopted the 'metro' concept
      even if there was a better charter presented at
      that time.

84

343. McNeely, Patricia G. "Road Council Started Government,"
      Columbia Record. February 6, 1971.

344. -----. "Expansion Laws Seen as 'Laughing Matter',"
      Columbia Record. February 8, 1971.

345. -----. "'Merger' Given Units' Blessing," Columbia
      Record. February 10, 1971.

346. -----. "Police Merger Issue Draws Various Views,"
      Columbia Record. February 11, 1971.

347. -----. "Ten Tax Districts like 'Puzzle'," Columbia
      Record. February 9, 1971.

348. -----. "Thoughts Varied on Merger Issue," Columbia
      Record. February 12, 1971.

349. "Mergers Reviewed for Local Units," National Civic
      Review. Vol. 61, No. 8, September 1972, pp. 417-
      419.

350. "Metropolitan County Recommended for Cleveland,"
      Metropolitan Area Problems News and Digest. Vol.
      I, No. 7, November-December 1958, p. 1.

351. "Metro Plan Loses in Knoxville," National Civic Review.
      Vol. XLVIII, No. 5, May 1959, p. 259.

352. "Metro Victory in Nashville," Metropolitan Area Problems
      News and Digest. Vol. V, No. 4, July-August 1962,
      p. 1.

353. "Metropolitan Government Proposed for Nashville, David-
      son County," Metropolitan Area Problems News and
      Digest. Vol. I, No. 4, April-May 1958, p. 2.

354. "Metro Police Proves Effective in Nashville," Metropoli-
      tan Area Problems News and Digest. Vol. VI, No. 5,
      September-October 1963, p. 7.

355. Miller, James N. " Metro - Toronto's Answer to Urban
      Sprawl," Reader's Digest. August 1967.

356. -----. "A City Pulls Itself Together," Reader's Digest.
      July 1967.

              A popularized version of the history behind
      the Nashville-Davidson County consolidation.
      While not detailed, the story does cover the high-
      lights of the consolidation effort and some of its
      results.

357. Morando, Vincent L. "Voting in City-County Consolidation Referenda," The Western Political Quarterly. Vol. XXXI, No. 1, March 1973, pp. 90-96.

Morando tests several variables against city and fringe voter support in a sample of 24 consolidation attempts between 1945 and 1970. He concludes that the number of charter-mandated elected officials is positively correlated to city and fringe "yes" votes, while pre-existing governmental fragmentation and central-city population dominance are negatively correlated to "yes" votes on the consolidation question.

358. -----, and D.K. Wanamaker. "Political and Social Variables in City-County Consolidation Referenda," Polity. Vol. 4, Summer 1972, pp. 512-522.

359. Morando, Vincent and Carl H. Whitley. "City-County Consolidation: An Overview of Voter Responses," Urban Affairs Quarterly. Vol. 8, No. 2, December 1972, pp. 181-203.

360. Myers, Phyllis. "Why did Indianapolis of All Places take a Step Toward Jurisdictional Metropolis?" City. Vol. 3, June 1969, pp. 37-39.

361. NACO Round Table. "City-County Consolidations, Separations, and Federations," The American County. November 1970.

362. "Nashville Commission to File Proposed Charter," Metropolitan Area Problems News and Digest. Vol. I, No. 3, February-March 1958, p. 7.

363. "Nashville Council Vetoes New Metro Charter," National Civic Review. Vol. XLIX, No. 3, March 1960, pp. 145-146.

364. "Nashville Metro Near," Metropolitan Area Problems News and Digest. Vol. V, No. 5, September-October 1962, p. 7.

365. "Nashville Thrives on a City-County Merger," Business Week. September 25, 1971, pp. 133-138.

366. "New City-County Charter Voted for Honolulu," Metropolitan Area Problems News and Digest. Vol. I, No. 5, June-July 1958, pp. 1, 4.

367. "New Mexico Cities Gain Home Rule," _Western City_.
January 1971.

368. "NO in Durham," _National Civic Review_. Vol. 63, No.
11, December 1974, p. 593.

369. Ostrom, V., C.M. Tiebout, and R. Warren. "The Organization of Government in Metropolitan Areas: A
Theoretical Inquiry," _American Political Science
Review_. Vol. LV, No. 4, December 1961, pp. 831-
842.

370. "Philadelphia Home Rule and City-County Charter under
the Pennsylvania Constitution," _University of
Pennsylvania Law Review_. Vol. 106, 1957, pp. 84-
97.

        A close, careful look at statutory provisions
    and court decisions surrounding the Philadelphia
    consolidated charter adoption in 1951. Considera-
    tion is given to consolidation effects upon
    former 'county' officers, personnel problems, and
    defining the role of the city-county vis-a-vis
    the Commonwealth of Pennsylvania.

371. Pinchbeck, R.B. "City-County Separation in Virginia,"
National Municipal Review. No. 29, July 1940, p.
467.

372. Pintarich, Paul. "Island State Well Suited for City-
County Consolidation," _The Oregonian_. November
22, 1970.

373. -----. "Planning Frustrated by Urban Sprawl," _The
Oregonian_. March 28, 1971.

374. "Portland Commission Releases Unification Study,"
Metropolitan Area Digest. Vol. XII, No. 6,
November-December 1969, p. 2.

375. "Portland Officials Study City-County Action," _Metro-
politan Area Problems News and Digest_. Vol. VI,
No. 2, March-April 1963, p. 7.

376. Prescott, Frank W. "Chattanooga Area Rejects Merger,"
National Civic Review. Vol. LIII, No. 7, July 1964,
pp. 385-386.

377. -----. "Memphis-Shelby County Reject Consolidation
Charter," _National Civic Review_. Vol. LX, No. 9,
September 1971.

378. "Propose Metro Plan for St. Louis," National Civic Review. Vol. XLVIII, No. 6, June 1959, p. 315.

379. "Public Health Consolidation Urged for Cleveland Area," Metropolitan Area Problems News and Digest. Vol. I, No. 4, April-May 1958, p. 8.

380. Reed, Henry E. "County Government in Oregon - A Growing Problem," National Municipal Review. Vol. 10, February 1921, p. 103.

381. "Regional Government is Needed - Now," Nation's Cities. December 1969, p. 27.

382. Rehfuss, John A. "Metropolitan Government - Four Views," Urban Affairs Quarterly. Vol. III, No. 4, June 1968.

383. "Report Proposes Merger of Governments in Charlotte Area," Metropolitan Area Digest. Vol. XI, No. 3, May-June 1968, p. 4.

384. "Reports and Recommendations of Metropolitan Surveys," Metropolitan Area Problems News and Digest. Vol. I, No. 1, October-November 1957, pp. 5-6.

385. "Reorganization Effort Failed in St. Louis," Metropolitan Area Problems News and Digest. Vol. V, No. 1, January-February 1962, p. 3.

386. Rich, A. McKay. "Portland OK's Metro District," National Civic Review. Vol. LIX, No. 7, July 1970, pp. 382-383.

387. "Richmond Considers City-County Merger," National Civic Review. Vol. LI, No. 10, October 1961, p. 493.

388. "Richmond, Henrico and the Merger Vote," The Virginian-Pilot. October 17, 1961.

389. "Richmond-Henrico Merger Rejected," National Civic Review. Vol. LII, No. 1, January 1962, p. 34.

390. "Rising Taxes on Homes, and the Search for the Way Out," U.S. News and World Report. July 12, 1971.

391. Rosenbaum, W.A. and T.A. Henderson. "Explaining the Attitudes of Community Influentials toward Government Consolidation," Urban Affairs Quarterly. Vol. 9, No. 2, December 1973, pp. 251-275.

A comparative study of the Jacksonville and Tampa consolidation attempts, which samples "community influentials" in both areas to determine support or opposition to consolidation. Their conclusions imply that substantive issues and charter provisions have little impact upon elites' alignments; that influentials' attitudes are not geared to well-defined groups' potential gains or losses under consolidation; and that the concept of dissatisfaction with previous governmental activities cannot be used as a predictor to identify consolidation proponents.

392. "St. Louis Advances to City-County Cooperation," Metropolitan Area Problems News and Digest. Vol. VI, No. 4, July-August 1963, p. 7.

393. "St. Louis Freeholders to Consider Two Plans," National Civic Review. Vol. XLVIII, No. 3, March 1959, p. 142.

394. "St. Louis to Vote on Consolidation," Metropolitan Area Problems News and Digest. Vol. V, No. 5, September-October 1962, p. 7.

395. Schaffer, Sheldon and Keith Bryant, Jr. "Is Consolidation the Answer?" County News/New County Times. Vol. 2, No. 5, June 8, 1973, p. 8.

The authors examine the concept of consolidation in the light of 12 criteria, including: Citizen involvement; service provision; responsiveness; accountability; equity; and competence. They conclude that a two-tiered consolidated government (such as UNIGOV/MINIGOV) would be superior to a single-tier structure, because of the citizen involvement generated at the grass-roots level in the two-tier system.

396. Schmandt, Henry J. "St. Louis Creates City-County Board," National Civic Review. Vol. XLVII, No. 7, July 1958, pp. 342-342.

397. -----. "St. Louis to Vote on Metro Plan," National Civic Review. Vol. XLVIII, No. 7, July 1959, pp. 359-361.

398. -----. "Study of Governments in St. Louis," National Civic Review. Vol. XLVII, No. 4, April 1958, pp. 179-181.

399. -----. "The Politics of Redesigning Community Govern-
        mental Structures," <u>Yale Law Review</u>. April 1968,
        pp. 52-67.

400. Scott, Thomas M. "Metropolitan Governmental Reorgani-
        zation Proposals," <u>The Western Political Quarterly</u>.
        Vol. XXI, No. 2, June 1968.

            Scott examines 18 governmental reorganization
        proposals, and constructs a scale of "radicalness"
        of governmental change. There are inconsistencies
        within the text, however, and the conclusions must
        be considered carefully in light of his text and
        the sample used.

401. Seago, Les. "Beaten in County," <u>The Chattanooga Times</u>.
        August 7, 1970.

402. Seltzer, Robert D. "Indiana Passes 'UNIGOV' Law,"
        <u>National Civic Review</u>. Vol. LVII, No. 6, June
        1969, p. 265.

403. Seplow, Stephen. "City, County Merger for Indianapolis,
        <u>The Des Moines Register</u>. January 18, 1970.

404. Seyler, William C. "Interlocal Relations: Cooperation,"
        <u>The Annals of the American Academy of Political and
        Social Science</u>. Vol. 416, November 1974, pp. 158-
        169.

405. Sikes, G.C. "The Advantages of City and County Consoli-
        dation," <u>The American City</u>. Vol. 21, September
        1919, p. 260.

406. "Sixty-Three Statutes Stress Urban Affairs," <u>Metropoli-
        tan Area Problems News and Digest</u>. Vol. VI, No. 4,
        July-August 1963, pp. 1-4.

407. Smallwood, Frank. "Modernizing Local Government: A
        Second Look," <u>Nation's Cities</u>. Vol. 5, No. 3,
        March 1967.

408. Smith, Alfred F. "San Francisco: Consolidation Pioneer,
        <u>National Municipal Review</u>. No. 30, March 1941, p.
        152.

409. "Something New Under the Georgia Sun," <u>Georgia County
        Government</u>. August 1970, pp. 22-42.

410. "State Legislative Acitivity to Affect Metropolitan Areas," <u>Metropolitan Area Digest</u>. Vol. XII, No. 3, May-June 1969, p. 3.

411. Stewart, Alva W. "Charlotte-Mecklenburg Reject Charter," <u>National Civic Review</u>. Vol. LX, No. 5, May 1971, p. 270.

412. ------. "Commission Drafts Charter for Charlotte-Mecklenburg County," <u>National Civic Review</u>. Vol. LIX, No. 11, November 1970, pp. 546-547.

413. ------. "Consolidation Vote Set for Charlotte-Mecklenburg," <u>National Civic Review</u>. Vol. LX, No. 3, March 1971.

414. "Study Commission Recommends City-County Consolidation," <u>Metropolitan Area Digest</u>. Vol. X, No. 3, May-June 1969, p. 3.

415. "Taming Metropolitan Growth," <u>Nation's Cities</u>. January 1968, p. 16.

416. Tanzler, Hans G. "Business is Solving a City's Problems," <u>Nation's Business</u>. July 1969, pp. 666-669.

417. "Task Force Recommends Consolidation of Louisville-Jefferson County," <u>Metropolitan Area Digest</u>. Vol. XIII, No. 2, March-April 1970, p. 4.

418. "Ten Super Cities - Home for One of Every Four Americans," <u>U.S. News and World Report</u>. August 2, 1971.

419. "Tennessee Votes on Charters this Summer," <u>Metropolitan Area Problems News and Digest</u>. Vol. V, No. 3, May-June 1962, p. 4.

420. "Texas County Consolidates Law Enforcement Functions," <u>National Civic Review</u>. Vol. 61, No. 1, January 1972, pp. 34-35.

421. "Texas Research League Evaluates Nashville Metro," <u>Metropolitan Area Digest</u>. Vol. IX, No. 3, May-June 1966, p. 4.

422. "Three Mayors Review Their Governments," <u>Nation's Cities</u>. November 1969, pp. 26-34.

423. "Twin Cities Area Council is Created," <u>National Civic Review</u>. Vol. LVI, No. 7, July 1967.

424. Twiggs, Margaret. "Richmond County and City of Augusta Race for Consolidation," <u>Georgia</u> <u>Government</u> <u>Magazine</u>. Vol. 16, April 1965, pp. 16-17.

425. Uhlman, Wes. "Seattle's Mayor Tackles the City-County Consolidation Bogeyman," <u>The</u> <u>Oregonian</u>. December 13, 1970.

426. "UNIGOV," <u>H.U.D.</u> <u>Challenge</u> <u>Magazine</u>. May 1971.

427. "Urban Problems Commission Reports on the American City," <u>Metropolitan</u> <u>Area</u> <u>Digest</u>. Vol. XII, No. 3, May-June 1969, p. 1.

428. "U.S. Chamber of Commerce Calls for Governmental Modernization," <u>Metropolitan</u> <u>Area</u> <u>Digest</u>. Vol. X, No. 4, July-August 1967, p. 1.

429. U.S. News and World Report Staff. "A Cure for City Blight - The Jacksonville Story," <u>U.S.</u> <u>News</u> <u>and</u> <u>World</u> <u>Report</u>. January 3, 1972, pp. 34-36.

430. "Virginia Acts on Metropolitan Commission's Recommendations," <u>Metropolitan</u> <u>Area</u> <u>Digest</u>. Vol. XI, No. 3, May-June 1968, p. 4.

431. "Virginia Study Commission Issues Report," <u>Metropolitan</u> <u>Area</u> <u>Digest</u>. Vol. XI, No. 1, January-February 1968, p. 1.

432. "Vote Pending: Consolidation Issue Up in Five Counties," <u>County</u> <u>News</u>/<u>New</u> <u>County</u> <u>Times</u>. Vol. 1, No. 9, December 15, 1972, pp. 7-8.

433. "Voter Reaction to Metropolitan Proposals Mixed," <u>Metropolitan</u> <u>Area</u> <u>Problems</u> <u>News</u> <u>and</u> <u>Digest</u>. Vol. II, No. 6, November-December 1959, pp. 1-2.

434. "Voters Approve New Consolidated Government for the City of Jacksonville," <u>Florida</u> <u>Municipal</u> <u>Record</u>. Vol. 41, September 1967, p. 5.

435. "Voters Turn Down Macon-Bibb County Charter," <u>National</u> <u>Civic</u> <u>Review</u>. Vol. XLIX, No. 9, September 1960, p. 441.

436. Walker, David B. "Regionalism: Defining the Term," <u>Public</u> <u>Management</u>. Vol. LII, No. 4, April 1970, pp. 4-7.

437. Warren, Robert. "A Municipal Services Market Model of
     Metropolitan Organization," *Journal of the American
     Institute of Planners*. Vol. XXX, No. 3, August
     1964.

438. ------. "Political Form and Metropolitan Reform," *Public
     Administration Review*. Vol. XXXIV, No. 3,
     September 1964, pp. 180-187.

439. "Washington Cities Gain at State Legislative Session,"
     Western City. July 1969.

440. Watson, Richard A. and John H. Romani. "Metropolitan
     Government for Metropolitan Cleveland: An Analysis
     of the Voting Record," *Midwest Journal of Political
     Science*. Vol. V, No. 4, November 1961.

441. Webb, Robert. "Merger Indy's 'Miracle'," *The Cincinnati
     Enquirer*. June 1, 1969.

442. White, Anthony G. "City-County Charter Defeated in
     Portland," *National Civic Review*. Vol. 63, No. 8,
     September 1974, p. 432.

443. ------. "City-County Commission Completes Portland
     Charter," *National Civic Review*. Vol. 63, No. 1,
     January 1974, pp. 34-35.

444. ------. "City-County Group Works on Charter," *National
     Civic Review*. Vol. LXI, No. 4, April 1972.

445. ------. "Differential Property Taxation in Consolidated
     City-Counties," *National Civic Review*. Vol. 63,
     No. 6, June 1974, pp. 301-305,+.

446. ------. "Metro Portland Saddled by 300 Governments,"
     Portland Commerce Magazine. Vol. LVI, No. 9,
     March 3, 1972.

447. ------. "Portland Group Drafting Charter," *National Civic
     Review*. Vol. 61, No. 10, November 1972, pp. 517-
     518.

448. ------. "Portland-Multnomah County Charter," *County
     News/New County Times*. Vol. 1, No. 9, December
     15, 1972, p. 8.

449. Whitwell, C.G. "The New Parish-City Government of
     Baton Rouge," *Southwest Social Science Quarterly*.
     December 1948.

450. Wicker, J. "North Carolina City-County to Vote on
      Charter," _National_ _Civic_ _Review_. Vol. 61, No. 9,
      October 1972, pp. 518-519.

451. Women Voters of Portland, League of. "November 3, 1970
      General Election," _Vote_. Vol. XIV, No. 2, n.d.

452. -----. "May 26, 1970 Primary Election," _Vote_. Vol.
      XIV, No. 1, n.d.

453. -----. "May 28, 1974 Primary Election," _Vote_. Vol.
      XVI, No. 1, n.d.

454. Wood, Thomas J. "City-County Merger Defeated in
      Florida," _National_ _Civic_ _Review_. Vol. 61, No. 7,
      July 1972, p. 361.

455. Woodman, Lyman L. "An Alaskan Metropolitan Government
      Would Combine the 15 Square Miles of the City of
      Anchorage with the 1500 Square Miles of Anchorage
      Borough," _American_ _City_. Vol. 81, September 1966,
      pp. 212, 214.

456. Young, Ed. "Nashville, Jacksonville, and Indianapolis
      Examined for Possible Lessons for Future,"
      Nation's _Cities_. November 1969, pp. 26-32.

457. Zeller, Florence. "Merger in the Blue Grass," _County_
      News/_New_ _County_ _Times_. Vol. 1, No. 9, December
      15, 1972, pp. 5-6, 11.

458. -----. "Consolidation: A Question of Service to
      Citizens," _County_ _News_/_New_ _County_ _Times_. Vol. 2,
      No. 1, February 1973.

          A brief report on the fourth NACO consolida-
      tion conference, held in Jacksonville. Zeller
      reports that consolidated-government mayors do
      not see their governments as ideal, nor would they
      recommend consolidation for all metropolitan areas.

459. Zimmerman, Joseph F. "Designing an Electoral System for
      a Consolidated Government," _Popular_ _Government_.
      March 1970, pp. 1-11.

460. -----. "Electoral Reform Needed to End Political Alien-
      ation," _National_ _Civic_ _Review_. Vol. LX, No. 1,
      January 1971, pp. 6-12.

461. -----. "Metropolitan Ecumenism: The Road to the Promised
      Land?" _Journal_ _of_ _Urban_ _Law_. Vol. XLIV, Spring
      1967, pp. 433-457.

462. -----. "Metropolitan Reform in the United States: An
             Overview," Public Administration Review.
             September-October 1970, pp. 531-543.

463. -----. "The Metropolitan Area Problem," The Annals of
             the American Academy of Political and Social
             Science. Vol. 416, November 1974, pp. 133-174.

464. Zukosky, Jerome. "Education, Housing Reform Offer New
             Regional Prospect," National Civic Review. Vol.
             61, No. 3, March 1972, pp. 128-135.

III. Legal Documents; Decisions

465. Alaska, State of. Alaska Statutes: Title 29, Chapter
          85, Sections 10-210. (Juneau: State of Alaska,
          n.d.).

466. -----. State Constitution of 1959, Article X, Sections
          3, 7. (Juneau: State of Alaska, 1959).

467. "Bardwell versus Parish Council," Southern Reporter,
          Second Series. Vol. 44, pp. 107-111.

              An attempt to prevent the election on city-
          parish consolidation on the grounds that the
          proposed issues to be voted on were illegal.
          Initially, an injunction was granted by a parish-
          level court, but the injunction was overturned by
          the state Supreme Court and the election was held.

468. "Beard versus City and County of San Francisco," Pacific
          Reporter, Second Series. Vol. 180, pp. 744+.

469. "Blum versus City and County of San Francisco," Califor-
          nia Reporter. Vol. 19, pp. 574+.

470. "Boston and Colorado Smelting Company versus Elder,"
          Pacific Reporter. Vol. 77, pp. 258-261.

              City and County of Denver attempted to levy a
          property tax immediately after its formation in
          1902, even though preceeding jurisdictions which it
          absorbed had levied such taxes only a month earlier.
          The Colorado Court of Appeals found against the
          City-County, and ruled that it had to wait 11
          months to levy its first property tax.

471. Baton Rouge, City and Parish of. The Plan of Government
          of the Parish of East Baton Rouge and the City of
          Baton Rouge. (Baton Rouge: City and Parish of
          Baton Rouge, 1947).

              The first consolidated charter to be adopted
          in the forty-year span that citizens were allowed
          to vote on such matters.

472. "Bryant versus Whitcomb," Federal Supplement. Vol. 306,
          No. 1P-70-C-115, U.S. District Court for Indiana.

473. California, State of. *An Act to . . . Establish the Boundaries of the City and County of San Francisco and To Consolidate the Government Thereof.* (Sacramento: State of California, April 19, 1856). Chapter CXXV, 7th Session.

This act clearly spells out the separation of a new San Francisco County boundary from the old boundary (to be coterminous with the city's), and renaming the remainder San Mateo County.

474. ------. *State Constitution of 1879, Article XI, Section 7.* (Sacramento: State of California, 1879).

475. "Carrow versus Philadelphia," *Atlantic Reporter, Second Series.* Vol. 89, pp. 496+.

476. City-County Consolidation Task Force, Portland Metropolitan Study Commission. *A Bill for an Act.* (Portland: The Commission, February 10, 1971).

477. "City of Douglas versus City and Borough of Juneau," *Pacific Reporter, Second Series.* Vol. 484, pp. 1040+.

A civic suit in which the City of Douglas sought to have the City-Borough charter ruled unconstitutional in calling for the dissolution of all cities in the borough into the City-Borough. Douglas lost, and was involuntarily merged into the unified government.

478. Charter Commission for South Norfolk and Norfolk County, Virginia. *Consolidation Agreement for the City of South Norfolk and Norfolk County, Virginia and Charter for the Consolidated City.* (Chesapeake: The Commission, 1961).

479. Colorado, State of. *Colorado Laws of 1901, Chapters 46, 68, 69, 70.* (Denver: Smith Brooks Printing Company, 1901).

480. ------. *State Constitution of 1876, Article XX, Sections 1-8.* (Denver: State of Colorado, 1876).

481. Columbus, Georgia, City of. *Charter of the Consolidated Government: Columbus, Georgia.* (Tallahassee, Fla.: Municipal Code Corporation, 1971).

Charter includes a code of ethics for public

officers and employees, differential taxing
districts, governance for a port commission, and
a race relations commission.

482. "Commonwealth ex. rel. Truscott versus City of Philadelphia," Atlantic Reporter, Second Series. Vol. 111,
pp. 136-146.

City of Philadelphia was restrained by the
court from abolishing a formerly-county position
and transferring the functions of that position to
another office, even though its home rule charter
gave it that power. As in the 1800s, following
Philadelphia's initial consolidation, the courts
begin to chip away at the consolidated government.

483. Consolidation Agreement and Charter for the Cities of
Nansemond and Suffolk, Virginia. (Suffolk: City of
Suffolk, 1972).

484. Denver, City and County of. Charter of the City and
County of Denver, Colorado. 1971 Revised, 1904
Basic. (Denver: City and County of Denver, 1971).

485. "Dortch versus Lugar," Northeastern Reporter, Second
Series. Vol. 266, pp. 25+.

The basic attack against the UNIGOV act's
constitutionality, and a challenge to the apportion-
ment of the City Council's makeup. The court found
in favor of UNIGOV.

486. "Dusch versus Davis," U.S. Supreme Court Reporter. Vol.
387, pp. 112+.

An attack on the proportional representation
used by Virginia Beach in seating its councilmen.
The court found for the city-county.

487. Florida, State of. Charter of Jacksonville: Chapter 67-
1320, Laws of Florida, 1967. (Tallahassee: State of
Florida, 1967).

488. ------. State Constitution of 1887, Article VIII, Sections
8, 9. (Tallahassee: State of Florida, 1887).

489. "Frazer et. al. versus Carr et. al.," Southwestern
Reporter, Second Series. Vol. 360, pp. 449-458.

The basic constitutional attack upon the metro-

politan government of Nashville-Davidson County.
Under particular attack was the State's authority
to delegate certain powers to the metropolitan
government; the metropolitan government's right to
abolish formerly-county offices; and the differential
taxing district plan. The court found for Nashville
on all charges.

490. Georgia, State of. Georgia Laws 1965, pp. 3354-3361.
      (Atlanta: The State, 1965).

491. -----. State Constitution of 1945, Article XI, Section
      1, Chapters 2-78. (Atlanta: The State, 1945).

492. Hampton, City and County of. The Charter and Code of
      the City of Hampton. (Hampton: The City, 1964).

493. "Hart et. al. versus Columbus, Georgia et. al.," South-
      eastern Reporter, Second Series. Vol. 188, pp. 422-
      429.

            A challenge to the manner in which Columbus
      officials sought to implement the consolidation
      provisions of state law, including the differential
      taxation plan. A close review was made of the
      service basis on which the plan was based, and
      found to be as fair as possible under the circum-
      stances.

494. Hawaii, State of. Hawaii Revised Statutes Chapter 70,
      Sections 1-123. (Honolulu: The State, n.d.).

495. Honolulu, City and County of. Charter, City and County
      of Honolulu, 1959: Act 261, Session Laws of Hawaii,
      1959. (Honolulu: The State, 1959).

496. "In Re: Consolidation of the Cities of Suffolk and
      Nansemond," Nansemond County Circuit Court.
      October 2, 1972.

            A local court's order that there be placed on
      the Suffolk city ballot the question of whether or
      not Suffolk should consolidate with Nansemond.

497. "In Re: Extension of Boundaries of City of Denver,"
      Pacific Reporter. Vol. 32, pp. 615+.

498. "In Re: Marshall," Atlantic Reporter, Second Series. Vol.
      62, pp. 30-33.

One of the continuing series of cases between 1860 and 1950 that continually chipped away at the power and authority of the Philadelphia consolidation. During this period Philadelphia had no home rule, and therefore no say over its own municipal affairs.

499. "In Re: Mayor, Etc. of City of New York," New York Supplemental Reporter. Vol. 53, pp. 875-877.

A challenge brought in 1898, the court found that the City of Greater New York had to pay retroactive fees to those who implemented the charter, and attempted to clarify administrative procedures found in the new charter.

500. Indiana, State of. Consolidated Government for Indianapolis as Provided by Indiana State Bill 543. (Indianapolis: Indiana State Senate, n.d.).

501. ------. Indiana Statutes, Chapter 173. (Indianapolis: The State, 1969). Pp. 357-448.

502. "Jackson versus Consolidated Government of Jacksonville," Southern Reporter, Second Series. Vol. 225, pp. 497+.

The main challenge to the constitutionality of the Jacksonville-Duval County merger. The challenge was based upon the state's restriction against passage of private acts, upon the use of differential taxation, and on other issues relating to the Florida constitution. The consolidated government won on all counts.

503. Johnson, Lee. Opinion Relating to Constitutionality of Taxing Differentials. (Salem, Or.: Oregon Attorney General's Office, May 17, 1971).

504. Juneau, City and Borough of. Home Rule Charter of the City and Borough of Juneau, Alaska. (Juneau: The Borough and City, 1970).

This charter provides for an ombudsman, election of councilmen on a district basis, recall procedures, service areas and differential taxation, the public school system, and an automatic, periodic review of the charter by a citizen's commission.

505. "Kahn versus Sutro et. al.," _Pacific Reporter._ Vol. 46,
     pp. 87+.

506. Kansas, State of. _Kansas Statutes Annotated, Chapter 12,
     Article 29._ (Topeka: The State, 1970).

507. Kentucky, State of. _House Bill No. 543._ (Louisville:
     Commonwealth of Kentucky General Assembly, 1970).

508. -----. _Kentucky Revised Statutes, Sections 67.190-.310
     and 81.410-.440._ (Louisville: The General Assembly,
     n.d.).

509. "Koelesch et. al. versus City of New York," _New York
     Supplemental Reporter._ Vol. 54, pp. 110-113.

     A case which provided the principle of succes-
     sion to debts of previous governments, wherein New
     York had to honor checks written prior to consolida-
     tion by one of the extinguished governmental bodies.

510. "Lennox versus Clark," _Atlantic Reporter, Second Series._
     Vol. 93, pp. 834-856.

     A decision found for the City-County of
     Philadelphia that the city-county government could
     abolish county offices and transfer functions under
     its new home rule charter, that old "county"
     employees automatically became "city" employees
     following consolidation, and that previously-
     elected "county" officials became bound by the
     provisions of the home rule charter.

511. Lexington Charter Commission. _Charter for the Lexington
     and Fayette Urban County, Kentucky._ (Lexington:
     The Commission, 1972).

     One of the few charters written in clear
     English for the layman, it provides for school
     district administration, water districts, automatic
     review of the charter on a periodic basis, and a
     code of ethics for employees and officials.

512. "Lindsey versus Denver," _Pacific Reporter._ Vol. 172,
     pp. 207+.

513. "Liter versus City of Baton Rouge," _Southern Reporter,
     Second Series._ Vol. 245, pp. 398+.

514. Louisiana, State of. _State Constitution of 1921, Article
     XIV, Section 3._ (Baton Rouge: The State, 1921).

515. Maryland, State of. _State Constitution of 1867, Article XIII, Section 1._ (Baltimore: The State, 1867).

516. "McKenna versus City of New York," _New York Supplemental Reporter_. Vol. 54, pp. 634-639.

517. "Metropolitan Government versus Allen," _Southwestern Reporter, Second Series._ Vol. 415, pp. 632-637.

   This case sets forth the liabilities which accrued to the Metropolitan Government of Nashville and Davidson County from the pre-existing governments. The main thrust has to do with tort liability, that is, governmental liability for failure to keep safe public facilities.

518. "Metropolitan Government of Nashville and Davidson County versus Poe," _Southwestern Reporter, Second Series._ Vol. 383, pp. 265-278.

   The Supreme Court of Tennessee found that under the metropolitan charter, the new civil service commission could not adopt a rule granting civil service status to all previous-government employees under the new government.

519. Michigan, State of. _State Constitution of 1963, Article VII, Section 27._ (Lansing: The State, 1963).

520. Minnesota, State of. _State Constitution of 1857, Article XI, Section 3._ (St. Paul: The State, 1857).

521. Missouri, State of. _Missouri Revised Statutes, Annotated Section 15744.5._ (Jefferson City: The State, n.d.)

522. ------. _State Constitution of 1945, Article VI, Sections 17, 30._ (Jefferson City: The State, 1945).

523. Montana, State of. _Revised Codes of Montana, Section 11-3406._ (Helena: The State, 1971).

524. ------. _Senate Journal of the 42nd Legislative Assembly of the State of Montana: Senate Bill 164._ (Helena: The State, 1971).

525. ------. _State Constitution of 1889, Article XVI, Section 7._ (Helena: The State, 1889).

526. "Montclair versus Thomas," _Pacific Reporter._ Vol. 73, pp. 48+.

527. Nashville and Davidson County. Charter of the Metropol-
      itan Government of Nashville and Davidson County,
      Tennessee. (Tallahassee, Fla.: Municipal Code
      Corporation, 1972.

          Includes as appendices authority for continu-
      ance of the Nashville Electric Power Board and for
      the Nashville Transit Authority.

528. Nevada, State of. Carson City Charter: Laws of 1969,
      Chapter 213. (Carson City: The State, 1969).

529. ------. State Constitution of 1864, Article IV, Section
      37. (Carson City: The State, 1864).

530. New Mexico, State of. State Constitution of 1912,
      Article X, Section 4. (Santa Fe: The State, 1912).

531. New York, State of. Consolidated Laws of New York
      Annotated, Chapter 378 of Laws of 1897, and
      "Alternate County Government Law", Article 12,
      Section 53. (Albany: The State, n.d.).

532. ------. State Constitution of 1895, Article XIII,
      Section 13. (Albany: The State, 1895).

533. Ohio, State of. State Constitution of 1851, Article X,
      Section 3. (Columbus: The State, 1851).

534. Oregon, State of. House Bill 1054. (Salem: The State,
      1971).

535. ------. Oregon Revised Statutes Chapter 199, Sections
      705-775. (Salem: The State, 1971).

536. ------. State Constitution of 1859, Article XI, Section
      2A, Paragraph 2. (Salem: The State, 1859).

537. Pennsylvania, State of. "First Class City Home Rule
      Act," Laws of Pennsylvania, Vol. 1, No. 155, 1949.
      (Harrisburg: The State, 1949).

538. ------. State Constitution of 1874, Article XIV,
      Section 8 and Article XV, Section 4. (Harrisburg:
      The State, 1874).

539. "People versus Sours," Pacific Reporter. Vol. 74, pp.
      167-189.

          This case was an attack against the constitu-
      tionality of the Denver consolidation, based on

proported irregularities in the printing of the
proposed amendment to the state constitution,
violation of the fourteenth amendment to the U.S.
constitution, and that the amendment presented
several subject matters within one measure. The
court found for the city-county on all counts.

540. "People versus Town Board," New York Supplemental
Reporter. Vol. 47, pp. 409-412.

A suit by the former Town of Hempstead to
overturn the New York City consolidation on the
basis that some of its citizens were refused the
right to vote on the measure due to a shift in
a river channel defining boundaries. The court
held in favor of the city-county.

541. "Pinchback versus Stephens," Southeastern Reporter,
Second Series. Vol. 484, pp. 327+.

This case was a suit brought to overturn the
enabling legislation passed by the Kentucky
legislature to allow the Lexington-Fayette County
consolidation. The court found in favor of the
state.

542. Philadelphia, City and County of. Philadelphia Home
Rule Charter Annotated. (Philadelphia: The City
and County, 1951).

543. "Portsmouth versus Chesapeake," Southeastern Reporter,
Second Series. Vol. 136, pp. 817+.

This suit, brought by the City-County of
Chesapeake, sought to halt an annexation instituted
by Portsmouth prior to the consolidation of South
Norfolk and Norfolk County. The court found in
favor of Portsmouth, and that city was allowed to
annex several square miles of the city-county.

544. "Robinson versus Briley," Southwestern Reporter, Second
Series. Vol. 374, pp. 382-386.

This was another in a series of personnel-type
lawsuits brought by formerly-"county" officers to
define their rights and responsibilities. This
particular case dealt with the County Trustee, to
whom all tax funds were tendered. The Metropolitan
Government sought to bypass this position, and its
stance was upheld by the court and in appeal.

545. "Rudd versus City of Columbus, Georgia," Southeastern
     Reporter, Second Series. Vol. 193, pp. 11-14.

         This action was brought to require the
         consolidated government to recognize a former
         officer's raise in pay prior to consolidation
         as an obligation of the new government. The
         Georgia Supreme Court upheld a lower court
         decision in favor of the officer.

546. Sitka Charter Commission. Home Rule Charter of the
     City and Borough of Sitka, Alaska. (Sitka:
     The Commission, 1971).

         Among other things, this charter provides for
         differential service and taxation areas within its
         jurisdiction.

547. "State ex. rel. Kemp versus City of Baton Rouge,"
     Southern Reporter, Second Series. Vol. 40, pp.
     477+.

548. Tennessee, State of. State Constitution of 1870,
     Article XI, Section 9. (Nashville: The State,
     1870).

549. Texas, State of. House Joint Resolution 22. (Austin:
     The State, November 3, 1970).

550. -----. 61st Legislature, 1968, Chapter 28. (Austin:
     The State, 1968).

551. -----. State Constitution of 1876, Article IX, Section
     3, Paragraph 6. (Austin: The State, 1876).

552. -----. Texas Statutes, Article 3, Sections 63 and 64.
     (Austin: The State, n.d.).

553. "Town of Montclair versus Thomas," Pacific Reporter.
     Vol. 73, pp. 48-50.

         This case led to a decision extinguishing all
         of the small towns in the territory taken in by
         the Denver consolidation.

554. "Traveler's Insurance Company versus Crome," Southern
     Reporter, Second Series. Vol. 223, pp. 227+.

555. Virginia, State of. Acts of Assembly: Chapter 9, 1952.
     (Richmond: The State, 1952).

556.   ----. Code of Virginia, Chapters 26 and 712.
       (Richmond: The State, n.d.).

557.   ----. The Virginia Concept. (Richmond: The State,
       n.d.).

558. Virginia Beach, City and County of. Charter for
       Virginia Beach, Virginia: Acts of Assembly, Chapter
       147, 1962. (Richmond: State of Virginia, 1962).

559. "Ware versus Cannon," Southern Reporter, Second Series.
       Vol. 248, pp. 19-24.

           This decision attempted to delineate areas of
       concern and control between the state legislature
       and the Baton Rouge Plan of Government, particularly
       as both relate to Louisiana election laws.

560. Washington, State of. State Constitution of 1889,
       Article XI, Section 16. (Olympia: The State, 1889).

561. "Webb versus Parish Council of East Baton Rouge, et. al.,"
       Southern Reporter, Second Series. Vol. 44, pp. 1074.

562. "Winter versus Allen," Southwestern Reporter, Second
       Series. Vol. 367, pp. 785-790.

           A decision in favor of the Nashville Metropoli-
       tan Government, ratifying charter-mandated duties
       to an officer different than the officer carrying
       out such duties under the pre-consolidated govern-
       ments. Such consolidated government-personnel
       clashes tend to fare 50-50 for each side in the
       courts.

IV. Miscellaneous Sources

563. Arthur Young and Company. _Letter_ to George M. Joseph, Chairman of the Portland-Multnomah County City-County Charter Commission, dated February 16, 1972. Subject: _Proposal_ _to_ _Provide_ _Management_ _Consulting_ _Services_ _to_ _the_ _Commission_.

564. Barron, Richard I. _Report_ _Concerning_ _Planning_ _within_ _the_ _Tri-County_ (Portland, Ore. area) _Area_. Unpublished paper, n.d.

565. Binion, Gayle. "A Study of Racially Discriminating Local Government Boundary Changes," _Draft_ _Chapter_, _White_ _Curtin_ _Project_. (San Deigo: California State University, n.d.).

566. Burgess, James V. _Letter_ to A. McKay Rich, Staff Director of the Portland Metropolitan Study Commission, dated August 7, 1970. Subject: _Columbus_, _Georgia_ _City-County_ _Consolidation_.

567. Carlson, Donald E., Executive Director of the Portland Metropolitan Area Boundary Commission. _Letter_ to Multnomah County Board of Commissioners, All Cities in Multnomah County, and others, dated March 7, 1972. Subject: _Boundary_ _Commission_ _Policy_ _on_ _Boundary_ _Changes_ _in_ _East_ _Multnomah_ _County_ _Prior_ _to_ _a_ _Vote_ _on_ _City-County_ _Consolidation_.

568. ------. _Letter_ to City Council of Lake Oswego, County Board of Commissioners, and others, dated March 7, 1972. Subject: _Boundary_ _Commission_ _Policy_ _on_ _City_ _of_ _Lake_ _Oswego_ _Annexations_ _in_ _Multnomah_ _County_ _Prior_ _to_ _a_ _Vote_ _on_ _City-County_ _Consolidation_.

569. Citizen's Committee. _Report_ _to_ _the_ _City_ _Council_ _of_ _Carson_ _City_ _and_ _County_ _Commissioners_ _of_ _Ormsby_ _County_. (Carson City: The Committee, December 1963). Mimeo.

570. Committee on Urban Government. _Minutes_ _of_ _Hearings_ _on_ _House_ _Bill_ _1054_. (Salem, Ore.: Oregon State House of Representatives, March 2, 9, and 25, 1971).

571. Lyons, W.E. _Why_ _Merger_? (Lexington: Committee to Insure Good Government, n.d.). Mimeo.

572. ------. _The_ _Lexington-Fayette_ _County_ _Merger_. (Lexington: Committee to Insure Good Government, n.d.). Mimeo.

573. League of Women Voters of Lexington. _Summary of the
     Charter for Urban County Government._ (Lexington:
     The League, 1972). Mimeo.

574. MacDougall, William R. _Consolidation: How is It
     Working?_ (Jacksonville: Speech before the
     National Conference on Consolidation, February 21,
     1973).

575. Multnomah County Employees' Union, Local No. 88.
     Will You Pay $6 to Help Protect Your Job? (Port-
     land, Ore.: The Union, 1971). Flier.

576. National Commission on Urban Problems. _Hearings
     before the National Commission on Urban Problems._
     (Washington, D.C.: U.S. Government Printing
     Office, 1968).

577. Onstine, Burton W. _Survey of Political Attitudes in
     Portland._ (Portland, Ore.: Portland State
     University, 1970). Unpublished study.

578. Seidl, Arline. _Kill the Bill #1054 - City-County
     Consolidation._ (Salem, Ore.: By the Author,
     March 25, 1971). Flier.

579. Select Committee on Consolidation, Senate Local
     Government Committee. _Minutes of Public Meetings._
     (Salem, Ore.: Oregon State Senate, May 5 and 13,
     1971).

580. Taxing District Study Committee. _Report to Mayor and
     Council, Consolidated Government, Columbus,
     Georgia._ (Columbus: The Committee, January 25,
     1971). Mimeo.

581. Webbon, Richard J. _Letter to Dr. Vincent Morando,
     University of Georgia, Athens, Georgia dated May
     8, 1970. Subject: Virginia Beach Consolidation._

582. White, Anthony G. _Impact of the City-County Consolida-
     tion Issue upon the Local Political Environment in
     the Portland Metropolitan Area._ (Vancouver, Wash.:
     Speech before the Pacific Northwest Political Science
     Association, April 27, 1974).

583. Zimmerman, Joseph F. _Political Alienation and the
     Electoral System._ (Portland, Ore.: Speech before
     the National Conference on Government, August 20,
     1970).

108

Numbers refer to bibliographic sources.

Numbers refer to bibliographic sources.

Lawrence, D.M.: 328

Lawson, B.G.: 102

Leiken, L.S.: 331

Lewis, T.P.: 332

Lineberry, R.L.: 335

Littlefield, N.: 109

Long, N.E.: 114

Lyons, S.R.: 116

Lyons, W.E.: 338, 571, 572

MacDonald, A.F.: 117

MacDougall, W.R.: 574

Macy, W.F.: 118

Maddox, R.N.: 119, 120

Makielski, S.J.: 121, 122, 339, 340

Mariner, E.E.: 123

Martin, R.: 125, 126

Martin, R.C.: 127

Maxam, W.P.: 305

Mayo, F.: 341

McDill, E.L.: 342

McElliott, M.: 132, 133

McLean, J.A.: 134

McNeely, P.G.: 343-348

Meltzer, J.: 16

Miller, J.N.: 355, 356

Moncrieff, J.A.: 17

Morando, V.C.: 357-359

Murphy, T.P.: 139

Myers, P.: 360

National Association of Counties: 142-144, 361

National League of Cities: 145

Nelson, H.J.: 146

Norton, J.A.: 151

Onstine, B.W.: 577

Ostrom, V.: 369

Paglin, M.: 153

Pinchbeck, R.B.: 371

Pintarich, P.: 372, 373

Podell, B.L.: 157

Prescott, F.W.: 376, 377

Reed, H.E.: 380

Rehfuss, J.A.: 382

Rhodes, D.G.: 169

Rich, A.M.: 386

Richardson, R.J.: 170

Ridley, J.C.: 342

Rogers, D.: 171

Romain, J.H.: 440

Rosenbaum, W.A.: 391

POSTSCRIPT

As it seems to be always with a text of this type, immediately after the preceeding text was prepared a new and excellant source on city-county consolidation appeared. Consequently, another listing should be added to the "Periodicals" section, and is highly recommended to the reader:

Morando, Vincent L. "The Politics of City-County Consoli-
    dation," National Civic Review. Vol. 64, No. 2,
    February 1975, pp. 76-81.

> Professor Morando has analyzed the voting
> patterns of consolidation referenda since 1949.
> He discusses voter support and opposition, the
> political process through which consolidations
> are attempted, and concludes that such referenda
> do not generate enough political organization to
> reach the broad base of voters necessary for
> adoption.

His tabular data point out two consolidation attempts omitted in this text, and also indicates that were it not for a concurrent-majority requirement (approval in the central city and in the unincorporated areas) there would be four more consolidated city-counties in the United States.